TWAYNE'S WORLD AUTHORS SERIES

A Survey of the World's Literature

Sylvia E. Bowman, Indiana University

GENERAL EDITOR

GREECE

Mary P. Gianos, Detroit Institute of Technology

EDITOR

Chariton

(TWAS 295)

TWAYNE'S WORLD AUTHORS SERIES (TWAS)

The purpose of TWAS is to survey the major writers —novelists, dramatists, historians, poets, philosophers, and critics—of the nations of the world. Among the national literatures covered are those of Australia, Canada, China, Eastern Europe, France, Germany, Greece, India, Italy, Japan, Latin America, the Netherlands, New Zealand, Poland, Russia, Scandinavia, Spain, and the African nations, as well as Hebrew, Yiddish, and Latin Classical literatures. This survey is complemented by Twayne's United States Authors Series and English Authors Series.

The intent of each volume in these series is to present a critical-analytical study of the works of the writer; to include biographical and historical material that may be necessary for understanding, appreciation, and critical appraisal of the writer; and to present all material in clear, concise English—but not to vitiate the scholarly content of the work by doing so.

Chariton

By GARETH L. SCHMELING
University of Florida

Twayne Publishers, Inc. :: New York

Library of Congress Cataloging in Publication Data

Schmeling, Gareth L
   Chariton.

   (Twayne's world authors series, TWAS 295. Greece)
   Bibliography: p.
   1. Chariton.
PA3948.C32S3   833'.01   73-14672
ISBN 0-8057-2207-6

Paul MacKendrick

Magistro Unico

Preface

Prose fiction was probably first heard on this planet when Cain and Abel ran up to Adam and asked him to tell them a story, perhaps of his adventures with the Snake, or of his heroic deeds in the army, or of his sacrifice of a rib. The earliest form of imaginative literature, which was surely oral, was possibly also prose fiction. The origin of prose fiction in oral form lies somewhere in man's unlighted past. Our interest here must, however, be confined to printed pages.

The rise of prose fiction in the ancient world is a phenomenon of such great consequence, in general to this study and in particular to Chariton, that a discussion of it at this time is imperative. Chariton stands at the very beginning of the history of prose fiction, for he wrote the earliest complete extant novel in the Western world. Chariton's novel, *The Adventures of Chaereas and Callirhoe,* surely had ancestors, contemporaries, and offspring; we will look at the most important of these. As a product of the collapse of Alexander's empire and the eastward thrust of powerful forces from Roman westerners, Chariton's world knows stresses of many kinds. Some of these come through Chariton's novel; others are forgotten or ignored in his fantasy world of fiction.

To understand best *The Adventures of Chaereas and Callirhoe* we must have some sense of the genre, developing and youthful as it is, in order to criticize and appreciate Chariton's work. We say that Chariton's work is a novel; this will require a more precise definition. On our way to this definition we will examine the rise of prose fiction in the ancient world and place Chariton firmly in this context. It is hoped that we can avoid the reproaches hurled at "mystical Germans who preach from ten 'til four" on the book of *Revelation,* but who insist on a beginning at *Genesis.*

Many critics of contemporary literature concede a preeminent place to the Greeks in the development of genres. Of the four main genres, epic, drama, elegy, and fiction, the Greeks get credit for originating and refining the first three. Fiction, i.e., prose fiction, allegedly arises in the modern world. Ian Watt (*The Rise of the Novel*, 1957) and Walter Allen (*The English Novel*, 1958) hold to this view. By the conclusion of this study we hope to have shown differently. But no polemics here.

The warm reception and unstinting service over the past several years from University Library, Cambridge, and the generous and wise counselings of Professor Mary Gianos are here acknowledged. The greatest debt, to teacher and friend, finds in the dedication small payment. All translations from the Greek are by the author. The reader's indulgence is requested: "Les traductions sont comme les femmes; si elles sont belles, elles ne sont pas fidèles; si elles sont fidèles, elles ne sont pas belles."

GARETH L. SCHMELING

Acknowledgment

Joseph Campbell, *The Hero With A Thousand Faces*. Bollingen Series XVII. Copyright © 1949 by the Bollingen Foundation. Reprinted by permission of Princeton University Press.

Contents

Preface

Acknowledgment

Chronology

Chronology

ca. 100 B.C.   Ninus Romance

A.D. 66   Petronius's *Satyricon*

117-138   Hadrian, Roman Emperor

ca. 125   Chariton

138-161   Antoninus Pius, Roman Emperor

161-180   Marcus Aurelius, Roman Emperor

ca. 180   Apuleius's *Metamorphoses*

ca. 200   Xenophon of Ephesus

ca. 225   Heliodorus

ca. 250   Longus

ca. 300   Achilles Tatius

ca. 300   Romance of Alexander

ca. 350   Apollonius of Tyre

ca. 400   Romances of Troy by Dictys and Dares

CHAPTER 1

Introduction to Chariton

I *Chariton and Classicists*

LIKE the famous Greek historians, Herodotus and Thucydides, Chariton begins his only extant work, *The Adventures of Chaereas and Callirhoe,* by introducing himself in the opening lines: "My name is Chariton of Aphrodisias, secretary to Athenagoras the lawyer." Chariton, the author, is the omniscient narrator, rarely intruding (like Henry Fielding) on the progress of the story; he is not a character in the action telling his own story, nor is his hero, Chaereas, a storyteller creation like Melville's Ishmael, nor a Dante-inspired guide through a world that might be. The reader will find in this novel, moreover, no hints toward an autobiography, unless the hero is an extension of Chariton's ego. The effective result of this self-effacement is to deny any modern student of ancient fiction a biography of its earliest extant writer. Chariton and his work come across the gulf from antiquity to us on one of the weakest paper (manuscript vellum and papyrus) bridges imaginable. The miraculous survival of Chariton's novel is a story of almost fairy-tale quality, not unlike the miraculous survivals of his own hero and heroine.

Chariton had chosen not to write in one of the established (by ancient critics) literary genres: epic, drama, and lyric. Since ancient critics did not bring into their purview Chariton's novel form, modern classical scholars have chosen also to ignore the genre. Up until very recent times classicists rarely trod new ground not previously covered by Aristotle in his *Poetics.* For those classicists primarily interested in imaginative literature Aristotle was regarded as some sort of magical lawgiver, a Moses who spoke to all and for all time. But Aristotle the philosopher was also to a greater or lesser degree a biologist, who thought like a biologist, but who in a fit of absentmindedness had turned to literature. For him literature was an object like a plant or a national constitution which could be best understood if properly dissected. At his best he was a literary pathologist.

The point of this slight polemical digression is a brief attempt at an explanation of why so little, or so much misguided, attention has been given to Chariton and ancient novels. The fault lies with the veneration of Aristotle (the prime mover) by the succeeding generations of critics and classicists who worshiped him but did not progress beyond him. Aristotle followed closely the doctrines of Plato and conceived of literature or genres in literature as an imitation (*mimesis*) of a universal pattern (*eidos*) whose variations the laws of nature strictly controlled. Literary genres were for him nothing more than imitations of Platonic Ideal Forms (*eide*), and as such were eternal, perfect, consistent, and unchanging. Aristotle made the analogy between literary forms and Platonic Forms (*eide*) by carefully analyzing literature and systematizing it. But in this action lies a tragic flaw. Aristotle analyzed and recorded only data from classical literature, i.e., Greek literature from Homer to the death of Euripides.

From this highly controlled experiment Aristotle's results were almost foregone conclusions. Greece was a small, closed society, within which stood city-states like Athens, which produced almost communal literature: a uniform society gave birth to a uniform literature which upon analysis was found to display uniform genres. Consequently, Aristotle concluded that behind the literary form stood one of Plato's immutable Ideal Forms. But literature was later larger than that of Athens or Greece, and every literary form did not grow or spring up from existing forms. The novel was not a product of Greece's closed society, and the prose narrative fictions which preceded the earliest novels were not dissected by Aristotle. Literary critics following Aristotle did not discuss the novel because it did not conform to aesthetic principles articulated by him: the novel was a prose form when fiction was relegated to poetry; each novel was in a class by itself and arose from the writer's literary imagination; it was not necessarily mimetic. For these and other reasons ancient novels were left unstudied.

There were occasional doctoral dissertations and articles on rare words, forms, and events in Chariton; but criticism of Greek prose fiction remained stagnant in backwaters. Then Erwin Rohde[1] in Germany and Samuel Wolff[2] in America took up the study of ancient novels, but Wolff did not discuss Chariton. Others followed these early pathfinders and began to look carefully at fiction, though as a rule many of these were more interested in the origins and peculiarities of romance than in the works themselves. The two Latin novels, on the other hand, Petronius's *Satyricon* and Apuleius's *Golden Ass*, have fared very well for many generations.[3] Perhaps only Longus's *Daphnis and Chloe*, handled so masterfully by William McCulloh,[4] has received just attention. The greatest contribution to ancient fiction to date is Ben Perry's *The Ancient Romances*,[5] against which every work in the field must be measured. Chariton suffered unjustly in respect to other Greek romance writers. The text of his work was not published until 1750, by which time the other romancers were well known and had become the standard for readers of that date. Also, for no good and valid reason, it was felt that Chariton was the last or latest writer of Greek romance, possibly even early Byzantine. Therefore, because he was not classical, many scholars assumed he was not good. While admitting that he had adopted a classical form for his work, these same scholars contradicted themselves by stating that he was not a classical author.

II *The Evidence for Chariton*

From the labors of archaeologists we have learned that there was a citizen of Aphrodisias named Chariton.[6] Also we know that a certain Athenagoras was a citizen.[7] Professor Joyce Reynolds of Newnham College, Cambridge, has been kind enough to keep us informed of up-to-the-minute news of the epigraphical "finds" at the archaeological "dig" at Aphrodisias. The fly in our carefully prepared ointment, however, is that we cannot positively identify Chariton the novelist with the Chariton from the inscription at Aphrodisias. If, on the other hand, we do not at least tentatively admit the reality of Chariton the novelist and identify him with the other, we will be forced to conclude that there were two Charitons in Aphrodisias and that they are not one and the same. Because our evidence is of the weakest kind, it seems best to choose the former solution, the simplest form of reasoning. Arguments for or against the chances of the name Chariton being a pseudonym lead nowhere.

Another tenuous attachment of the name of Chariton to reality is a scathing comment by the rhetorician Philostratus (second-third century A.D.), who addresses a letter (no. 66) to a certain Chariton. (In a society which did not lay any stress on listing, at every turn, the last, first and middle names of every person, it is difficult to identify this person or that.):

> You believe that succeeding generations will remember your writings when you are dead? What will writers be when they are dead, if we consider that they do not exist while they are alive?

This is the kind of judgment Philostratus would have made about Chariton the novelist. He would not have approved of the Greek style of *The Adventures of Chaereas and Callirhoe.* The exact reasons for this dislike we will discuss later. Though Philostratus's statements do not single out our Chariton from other possible writers of the same name, we are inclined to believe that Philostratus is here denigrating our Chariton and his novel.

For the name of his heroine Chariton chose Callirhoe ("Lovely Stream"), a not infrequent name in antiquity. When he did so, did he also assume the name of a girl around whom many myths and legends had sprung up and who was in fact the heroine of a small corpus of literature? Did there exist at that time a cycle of stories concerning the exploits of Callirhoe and her famous father, Hermocrates? No such stories are extant today. Some scholars hold that Chariton did not create his own story but rather put together a series of adventures of Callirhoe. But there is little possibility that Chariton decided to write about Callirhoe because she and her adventures had some popularity and vogue. There is, however, reason to suppose that myths about Hermocrates were perennial favorites, especially in Syracuse, where in 413 B.C. he led the Syracusans to victory over Athens. In addition to Chariton, only Persius (d. A.D. 62), the Roman poet, mentions Callirhoe as a literary creation. In the very last line of his first satire Persius says with a sneer:

For undiscriminating gentlemen I would recommend *Callirhoe* for the afternoon.

Callirhoe here is some type of literary production. Weinreich[8] suggests the possibility that Persius is alluding to the novel of Chariton, which at that date (A.D. 62) would have been regarded as light reading after lunch. If Weinreich is right, the latest possible date for the composition of this novel must be A.D. 62, much earlier than the presently accepted date. Again the evidence is tantalizing but inconclusive

III *The Home of Chariton*

Chariton begrudgingly put out two meagre bits of information about himself. We learn from his own pen that he lived in Aphrodisias and that he was secretary to a lawyer named Athenagoras. Though the reader might not recognize him, Chariton hoped the reader would have heard about Athenagoras. As fate would have it, Athenagoras was known only locally, and nothing further can be said of him. To be chosen for the position of secretary to a lawyer, a man had to be literate and skilled in writing and diplomacy. It is important to notice and to remember that Chariton was not the lawyer, the narrowly trained and well-paid rhetorician. He held a minor position, but one of which he was obviously very proud. Many other famous writers held the position of secretary, though under more illustrious employers. We need think only of Suetonius, Milton, or Goethe.

In the great Roman Empire of the first-second century A.D., Aphrodisias played an interesting and colorful but not vital role politically or economically. In this small pool Chariton and Athenagoras were big fish. The social status of Chariton did not affect his talent as a writer or doom his literary product to oblivion somewhere between his death and the two thousand years which have elapsed since then.

The discovery and recovery of Chariton's city of Aphrodisias have elements of romance which could have found a home in *The Adventures of Chaereas and Callirhoe*. Much of the past interest in Chariton's work is similar to the interest in the archaeological work at Aphrodisias. Gilbert (of Gilbert and

Sullivan fame) called it a "fascination frantic in a ruin that's romantic." For the past ten years Professor Kenan Erim, a Turk, has been excavating the city of Aphrodisias under the sponsorship of the National Geographic Society. Located in Turkey's rugged Anatolian hill country (south central Turkey), an area known to Chariton's contemporaries at Caria, Aphrodisias lies about one hundred and thirty-five miles southwest of Izmir, at a height of approximately eighteen hundred feet above sea level. The results of Professor Erim's work are splendidly done up with drawings, maps, color photographs, and authoritative text in the *National Geographic*[9] and are available to anyone, even those who do not have easy access to good archaeological libraries.

It appears that the city of Aphrodisias has a long history, having been inhabited first in the third millennium B.C. by unidentified peoples, of which Chariton was proud. By analogy with other Anatolian prehistoric sites we can assume that the chief deity of this city was the Great Mother, known here as Cybele, the powerful force representing the female influences. By 205 B.C. Cybele had a temple as far west as Rome. From archaeological evidence found in the precinct under the temple of Aphrodite of Aphrodisias it appears that the inhabitants had built some shrine to Cybele as early as 700 B.C. In the succeeding generations Cybele gained influence through a continuing process of syncretism and assumed many of the functions of other female deities. Regardless of the actual name, the Great Mother reflected the aspects of a coherent group of goddesses.

Following the armies of Alexander the Great in the latter part of the fourth century B.C. came Greek settlers, administrators, and (important for our study) religious rites, customs, and deities. Greek became the language of the educated classes. Though the functions remained constant, the Great Mother was now called Aphrodite, retaining some of her Eastern aspects and borrowing others from Western religious experience. Aphrodite was the most important deity in this new Asiatic-Greek city, and became the eponymous goddess when the city's name was changed from Ninoe (after a deity named Nina, similar to Ishtar) to Aphrodisias. The Greek goddess of love became the symbol for the existence and power of the city.

The great marble Ionic temple built in the first century B.C. to this imported Greek goddess stood as the most important civic monument in the city. Even the Roman dictator Sulla in 82 B.C., according to the historian Appian, made offerings to the Carian Aphrodite. By the late second century A.D. Aphrodisias was one of the wealthiest and brightest cities in Asia Minor. Art works from here could be found in most cities of the Roman Empire. The inhabitants of the city attributed this good fortune to the aid of Aphrodite who oversaw love, fertility, wealth, and good fortune. She was ever at the conscious level in the minds of most Aphrodisians; when the citizens succeeded in any form, Aphrodite was directing or acting the part of Lady Luck. In Chariton's *The Adventures of Chaereas and Callirhoe* Aphrodite is the prime mover of the plot, and in a very real sense the whole novel is a tribute to her power and an aretology of her mysterious wonders.

As we discuss the novel of Chariton it will be important for us to keep ever in mind the importance of Aphrodite to the inhabitants of Aphrodisias. The city in its totality obviously meant much to Chariton. It is reasonable to assume that the magnificent temple of Aphrodite suggested the opening scene in the novel and that the elegant theatre and the productions in it gave Chariton his fine sense for the dramatic. An absolute witness to the strength of Aphrodite and to the devotion of her followers in Aphrodisias is the fact that the city was one of her last bastions of support in the ancient world. Many will be surprised to learn that under the Roman (Byzantine) Emperor Justinian (A.D. 527-565) the worship of Aphrodite was alive and well in Aphrodisias, two hundred years after Christianity had been established as the state religion and pagan rites had been banned.

IV   *Language and Style of Chariton*

Short of quoting long passages of original Greek prose from Chariton's pen, it is a difficult task to illustrate well the style of that language employed by Chariton. To begin we can make several broad generalizations which would be immediately apparent to the Greek reader: Chariton had adopted a style called

Menippean, which was a mixture of prose and verse; Chariton's Greek belongs to the Asianic (as opposed to Attic) mode of rhetorical expression. The prosimetric form, called Menippean after its originator, the cynic philosopher Menippus of Gadara (fl. 250 B.C.), was used frequently by satirists like Varro (116-27 B.C.; *Saturae Menippeae*). In his novel of A.D. 66 called the *Satyricon*, Petronius employed this form, and it may be that this precedent-setting work encouraged Chariton also to utilize the prosimetric structure. The Menippean mode became very popular in late antiquity.

Speaking in an absolutely coherent manner about the Greek language employed by Chariton is also not an easy undertaking. Generally, however, he is classified among the writers in the Asianic school, a somewhat derogatory designation when compared with the Attic school. Asianic Greek, as seen by contemporary classicists, is not a positive or pure style, but rather a degradation, almost an antithesis, of the perfection of Attic style. The writers of Attic dialect are the famous Greek tragedians, plus Aristophanes, Plato, Isocrates, and Demosthenes. Attic Greek was that dialect spoken and written in the district surrounding the city of Athens. It was a small district, but because of the power of Athenian arms which gave Athens the hegemony in much of the Greek world, Attic Greek became the most influential. In addition to Athenian might spreading the Attic dialect, Athens produced a succession of magnificent writers whose style, diction, and dialect were widely imitated. The Attic dialect spread to Asia Minor and was there tempered by the local Ionic dialect and Ionicized.

Several forces were at work in the late fifth century B.C. to chip away at the supremacy of Attic Greek and to bring it and many other dialects of Greek into some kind of uniformity. Athens lost her hegemony over the Greek world in 406 B.C. to Sparta, and in the next century Macedonia established its leadership over the same world. Alexander destroyed the small, individual city-states, and then consolidated and unified Greece under his own control. Various Greek dialects were thus also absorbed, unified, and leveled into one language to serve the new and larger empire which stretched from Greece to India. Attic Greek lost some of its striking peculiarities as it blended into other dialects, which for their part lost peculiarities also. Political realities thus had a strong impact on shaping the new language. Alexander's empire needed a common language to aid trade and commerce and also to give the far-flung state some cohesion. This new language was the Koine Greek.

A second force at work to change classical Attic style was the new kind of rhetoric, in reality a reaction against the carefully constructed periodic and symmetrical style of writers like Isocrates. The style of Greek popular in Asia Minor and called Asianic replaced the earlier Attic mode. Beginning already with Xenophon of Athens (b. 430 B.C.) and continuing with Menander (b. 342 B.C.) Attic style lost some of its purity, while retaining its lucid simplicity (*apheleia*). Slowly but surely the language became more lavish and emotional, and a linguistic laxity appeared in certain areas, like the disuse of the optative mood, disappearance of differences between the perfect and aorist tenses, and the disappearance of the dual number. Such changes are not evident in all authors, nor did they come about quickly, or in all social classes at the same time. The upper classes were divided between an adherence to the old and a love of the avant-garde. The lower classes spoke and wrote a level of Greek which is best illustrated by the Koine Greek of the New Testament. The best of the new Asianic rhetoricians encouraged a style of Greek which was not periodic but rather a quick succession of short clauses and an accretion of words and phrases which agitated the reader by sense and sound. It appealed to the tragic and dramatic. The net result was a disquietude and restlessness, unfamiliar to those of the earlier rhetorical training and school.

To this Asianic action there was in turn and in time a reaction. It began in the first century B.C. and continued for many years, finding perhaps its most famous proponent in Philostratus (fl. A.D. 200). This reaction to Asianism took the form of neo-Atticism, a kind of Attic style which went beyond even the carefully structured Attic of fifth-century B.C. Athens. This neo-Atticism was a completely artificial language with little in common with contemporary spoken Greek, even that spoken by the upper classes. Adherents to neo-Atticism searched early Attic writers for rare words, for example, and sprinkled their own works with the same. This movement also revived the use of the optative mood.

Actions, reactions, and then counterreactions left the Greek language at the time of Chariton (or shortly after Chariton, if we place him in the late first or early second century A.D.) with three distinct levels: (1) on the left wing was the Koine, used by the common people and the most widespread of all the levels; certain parts of Koine Greek were closely tied to the Asianic style and were surely too literate for everyday commerce; (2) on the right was the highly stylized and artificial neo-Attic Greek, advocated by certain rhetoricians; (3) in the middle was a Greek called Hellenistic, which preserved certain parts of Attic Greek but adopted also many innovations of Asianism; Chariton belongs, we feel, to this persuasion. Only in this schematic outline, however, are the three levels so neatly defined. The various writers' social classes, place of birth, rhetorical training, and personal temperament tend to obscure our boundaries and blend our divisions.

Chariton's Greek is pleasant and lucid, and rarely if ever draws the reader up short and forces him to reread the sentences just gone over. The simplicity and straightforwardness of his Greek is aided by the unaffectedness of the story he tells. His narrative, having no deep and dark meanings, stands transparent to the Greek reader. But there are flavors to Chariton's Greek which are hard to lump together and explain in a mere word or two. He quotes Homer's original epic dialect frequently and uses many epic devices in telling his story. This reflects an age Chariton never knew. Few pages go by without Chariton imitating the three great Greek historians, Herodotus, Thucydides, and Xenophon, but he avoids carefully the hiatus (the gap that occurs when a word ending with a vowel is immediately followed by a word beginning with a vowel) so readily admitted by Thucydides. In avoiding the hiatus he follows Isocrates. In his *clausulae* ("rhythmical sentence endings") Chariton carefully imitates Attic writers, but many other of his grammatical usages belong to the Koine: he uses many old words in the new ways of the Koine and with the changed meanings of the Koine. Many of the specific instances of Koine Greek usage have been nicely assembled for us by Antonios Papanikolaou.[10] Chariton

presents us with an interesting combination of Greek simply
written but highly allusive to earlier classical Attic authors.

A word should be added here about the simplicity of Chariton's
Greek compared with the so-called simplicity (*apheleia*) of the
neo-Attic writers, who are usually referred to as members of
the Second Sophistic movement. Chariton's simplicity of language
arises from his straightforward approach to his subject, and
from the fact that his literary prose stands relatively close to
the spoken middle-class Greek of the day. The simplicity of the
neo-Atticists is artificial, attempting to conceal its ornateness,
and no longer really simple or natural, whereas that of Chariton
retains a kind of naiveté. The rhetoricians of the Attic revival
are so eager to recapture the lucid simplicity of someone like
Xenophon that they go beyond Xenophon and write a Greek
that is more precious than simple, more affected than restrained.

Chariton's love of the dramatic leads him toward the theatrical
and the emotional, qualities admired by the Asianic school. In
the language itself he avoids the dual number (as opposed to
singular and plural numbers), the nominative absolute, and
hiatus, and admits the optative mood only rarely. In a mere
five instances does Chariton pause to ask a rhetorical question,
but he does take many occasions to summarize and recapitulate
old material. Frequently, there are long breaks in the action for
monologues or soliloquies, and Book 4 is punctuated by several
rhetorically inspired letters. The typical sentence in Chariton
runs along smoothly, being built up of short phrases which are
usually not tied tightly together (*asyndeton*) and giving the
impression of a lively and impassioned narration. While the
prose of Chariton resembles spoken Greek much of the time,
Chariton shows a real ability and preference for fine Attic phras-
ing. In the total structure of the novel we observe that the progress of the plot is direct from start to finish without any episodic
building blocks or minor climaxes or subclimaxes. Within given
sections of the total structure Chariton employs a kind of stencil
to paint his action and scenery. Though the time, place, and
characters change, the reader is left with the impression that
he has seen (or read) this scene before. The net result is that
the style of narrative, which the author absorbed in school but
never quite made his own, possesses a kind of stiffness.[11]

CHAPTER 2

Rise of Prose Fiction
in the Ancient World

WE live in a reflective and not highly original age in which
criticism is a higher art form than primary art, in which
the study of art has been reduced to a science, and in which
criticism is a well thought out system of classifications based on
methods and procedures of "classic" authors. Our period of
classic criticism is a self-conscious age. Throughout our consideration of Chariton's *The Adventures of Chaereas and Callirhoe*, we will try to keep always in mind the realization that we
have in front of us a work of art removed from us in time by
2000 years. Regardless of our frequent scientific or scholastically
narrow digressions, the reader will hopefully find a balanced
approach to the virtues and faults of Chariton's work.

I *Rise of Prose*

Prose fiction to most readers means the novel, perhaps the
dominant literary form of the past many generations. Contemporary prose fiction subsumes under itself not only the novel
but also romance, satire, humor, travel stories, detective stories,
science fiction, utopias, and certain long essays. We have a
surfeit of imaginative prose forms, and only on rare occasions
do we see poetry. In the ancient world this situation was reversed,
and in addition imaginative literature was subsumed under
poetry. Prose was reserved for history, science, and philosophy.
When prose fiction evolved (shades of Darwin!) in the ancient
world, its resultant offspring was the novel or romance. The non-
imaginative literature forms like history, philosophy, and science
already existed at the birth of the novel. Satire belonged to
poetry; science fiction, detective stories, and humor in prose

26

never existed in the ancient world as we know them; travel stories came closer to the ancient novel. Imaginative literature in Greece and Rome rode the vehicle of poetry until sometime in the second-first century B.C. when, at one level at least, a part of it switched to prose. This change from poetry to prose for fiction is one of the most significant developments for ancient, medieval, and modern literatures.

From the time of Homer (ca. 800 B.C.) to the rise of the middle and lower classes in the early Roman Empire, literature, i.e., poetry for the most part, was the domain of the wealthy upper classes. With the stability brought about by Roman law and order, trade and business flourished; hand-to-mouth existence fell on a very small percentage of the people. For some people in these lower strata released time or recreational time was spent with prose literature. Poetry, generally speaking, is a literary vehicle requiring careful study, contemplation, close attention to aesthetic detail, and a solid background in literary history. Poetry thus fits well among the upper classes and people of leisure. It is reasonable to assume with Thorstein Veblen[1] that poetry belongs to the leisure class because, aside from aesthetic value, it is openly useless. Prose, on the other hand, is the language of the common man because it is a useful medium, quickly grasped, though the comprehension may be superficial. In prose the lower classes found or created their level of literature. It is worthwhile to point out at this time that the novels written in Latin prose are more comic and satiric than those in Greek literature, for the literary men in Rome in the first centuries B.C. and A.D. operated in, and were confined by, various pressures to traditional lines that said that comic and satiric narratives were accepable in prose while serious and idealistic work should be reserved for poetic vehicles. But writers in the far-flung Hellenized world of Alexander's old empire were under few literary confinements. A literary man like Chariton had freedoms in composition which were not enjoyed at Rome. If Chariton chose to write, as he did, imaginative and idealistic literature in prose, he could easily escape critical censure that writers in Rome could not. The Latin writers of novels, Petronius and Apuleius, aimed their works of comedy and satire at the upper class audiences; Chariton, like the writers of the New Testament, directed his novel at the lower classes. As Ben Perry noted so aptly, "the literary language of the poor-in-spirit was not Latin but Greek."[2]

According to ancient literary convention, if an author wrote in prose, he was writing at first sight a type of history and not imaginative literature. But the human spirit will always find a way out of such restrictions. The historians Herodotus and Xenophon, for example, were perhaps as fond of imaginative stories as of history, and released creative energy by placing fictionalized short stories within their histories. These beginnings finally degenerated in other authors to a form of writing called "tragic history," i.e., the entire work was the product of imagination but continued to be passed off as history. Variants within this are to be found in histories of all kinds: one writer relates a purely imaginative story but claims to have found it in some library or other and by implication passes it on as a true history; another reports a story that some honest foreigner told him; a third writer sets down a story worth reporting because, though it is fabulous in nature, he himself saw all the events described.

To the ancient literary critic fiction belongs under poetry. Prose fiction stood as a type of bastard in ancient literature, an embarrassment, a genre which somehow did not seem to belong. In commenting on the role of the historian in *Poetics* 9 Aristotle says that it is his concern to describe what actually happened, but it is the function of the poet to tell what might happen or even (*Poetics* 24) to tell lies. Prose was thus taken to be the vehicle for narratives of reality, poetry the vehicle for imaginative literature. And so it was apparently accepted that to write imaginative literature in prose, since imaginative literature was regarded as poetic in nature, was to violate some formal or ideal principle of aesthetics. Such flaunting of aesthetics doomed prose fiction to a lesser position in the hierarchy of literary forms.

It is difficult to learn whether narrative prose fiction grew up outside the circle of fashionable literature and never sought entrance within the magic circle, or, seeking admission to the inner orbit of established classical works, it was shut out. Regardless of the methods or reasons for exclusion, ancient novels make up a kind of underground literature. A reading of the three Latin and five Greek novels will illustrate to the perceptive student that these works differ from the standard corpus of what we mean by *classical* literature: classical literature was written for the upper classes, novels for the popular taste of the inarticulate and intellectually undisciplined readers; classical literature supposedly displays balance, unity, proportion, restraint, and what Winckelmann called "noble simplicity and quiet grandeur," much of which classical novels seemingly disregard. This lack of concern for classical norms is most prevalent among the writers of Greek novels, who apparently came from the middle classes and spoke to an audience of the middle classes. One ill-defined form of writing which used the vehicle of prose from the time of Xenophon and Isocrates on (fifth-fourth centuries B.C.) was biography. Masquerading as history, biography soon became romanticized, idealized, and almost a type of fiction. Xenophon's *Cyropaedia* (*The Education of Cyrus*) is much closer to an historical novel than to biography or history. Xenophon made Cyrus a creation of fiction similar to the incredible and romantic figure of Alexander the Great in the later fictionalized biography by Pseudo-Callisthenes. Such romantic leaders have a great appeal among the masses. Chariton, perhaps consciously, imitated this accepted form of fictionalized biography; once he discovered a pretext, the rest was invention.

In the early second century A.D. when Chariton began to write his novel, another force was gaining momentum and giving respectability to prose as a vehicle for imaginative literature. This force was the so-called Second Sophistic, a movement which cultivated the high art of epideictic oratory, i.e., oratory for displaying versatility, craftsmanship, and virtuosity; oratory for the sake of oratory, show pieces. Each orator could choose the subject matter for his dramatic performance from a wide range of sources: history, myth, and his own imagination. Using these sources as he pleased or finding in them an outline suitable to his style, the orator would attack or defend individuals or movements. The resultant overblown, rhetorical prose was never intended to serve any useful function, that is, as a vehicle for history or science, other than the entertainment of its audience.

Epideictic oratory should be described as a secondary, not primary, art form. The orations were designed to be intellectually pleasing; their importance in courtrooms and legislative assemblies had passed away as the power of Greece passed on to Rome and the influence of the orally gifted gave way to a complicated bureaucracy. Through the influence of this Second Sophistic movement, prose for unhistorical purposes gained in stature and acceptance. It was respectable for a sophist to construct an entire rhetorical piece from fictional elements without apology, provided there was some purpose of education or edification of the audience.

The next step, where the sophist wrote or spoke merely to entertain his audience, was also an easy one. Fictional prose had been permitted in small doses within historical and philosophical works, but never as an end in itself. But now in the Second Sophistic we can see that such a change is welcome, if set within the framework of rhetorical showpieces. Certain sophists, quick to grasp this new outlet for their abilities, began to write fictional prose solely for entertainment: the last three of the five Greek novelists, Longus, Heliodorus, and Achilles Tatius, were all member of the Second Sophistic movement and wrote prose fiction in such a way that these would above all display their rhetorical abilities.

II *The Reading Public*

The structure of society in the ancient Greek and Roman world was closed, with little or no upward mobility. Literature of all kinds including poetry and later prose, which is extant today, was written for, and reflected the sentiments and feelings of, the upper classes. Those writers born in the lower ranks of this stratified society and showing literary inclinations and promise of greatness were taken into various artistic circles or coteries and supported by interested wealthy nobles. What we have of classical literature is almost exclusively the literature of these upper classes; from the lower and middle classes we have almost nothing. The largest source or best library of materials of lower-class literature from the ancient world is Pompeian graffiti.

For the nobility and the wealthy of antiquity all sorts of literature were available; wealthy men had fantastic libraries, as we
can see from Pompei and Herculaneum, and the libraries of
Pliny the Younger. It is interesting to examine the accesses
to literature available to the poor. In the fourth century A.D.
Rome alone had twenty-nine libraries, and many more were
scattered around the empire. Borrowing and browsing were
permitted in state libraries. Of course books were freely exchanged between owners, and booksellers sold to all customers
with cash.[3] Bookstores and the book trade were well-established
in the reign of Augustus (27 B.C.-A.D. 14) and moved to the
provinces in the first century B.C. Around such bookstores literary circles formed and men of all kinds of letters rubbed elbows,
as the "Lost Generation" of American writers would do many
centuries later in Sylvia Beach's bookstore in Paris.

From the masses of inscriptions which survive from Pompei,
we can be reasonably sure that in A.D. 79 there was a sizable
portion of Pompeian citizens who could read. Notices intended
for all classes of people were written, circulated, and meant to
be read; the government had all types of information copied
and circulated throughout the empire. The problem of whether
or not the average citizen bought books remains. One possible
solution: because of cheap slave labor a publisher would have
one man dictate a text to hundreds of scribes writing at one
time, and so, like a modern press, produce hundreds of copies
per day.[4]

Though it is a speculative matter, we can try to investigate
the price of books in Rome and attempt to discover whether
or not the common man could afford them. The cost of an
average book in Rome was about four sesterces (one denarius).
We cannot establish a perfect equivalent, but we do know
that a man in the lowest class earned about two hundred sesterces (fifty denarii) per year.[5] If our average man bought one
average book per year, he would have to spend one-fiftieth of
his annual income. In the United States the average worker
probably earns twenty-five dollars a day, but would buy few
books costing as much as one-fiftieth of his annual income. On
the other hand some average workers do purchase sets of ency-
clopedias or large, ornate Bibles costing many hundreds of

dollars. So it is perhaps reasonable to assume that some members of the lower (but not lowest) income groups would have purchased books. If we consider that the individual might purchase a work written on papyrus, we should note that an average roll of papyrus cost a little more than one day's income.[6] If we move up the economic ladder and consider that a centurion in the army of Domitian (Roman emperor A.D. 81-96) received five thousand denarii per year, we can see that with a monthly salary of four hundred and twenty-five denarii, he could well afford several books per month.[7] Papyrus rolls would not withstand second-hand book trade because they frayed easily and rotted in damp places; expensive parchment (made from sheepskin) survives thousands of years of wear.

Taken together, the libraries, book and papyrus trade, and private circulation of books, had at best only a moderate impact on the lowest classes. But as we look up the economic ladder, we find more and more purchasing power and probable use of books. If any literary productions came to the lowest class, it was by way of recitations done by traveling storytellers, inexpensive or state financed plays, or cheap papyrus copies of works like Chariton's. That Chariton was read and known from copies of his work on cheap papyrus as far away as Egypt is attested by the discovery of fragments in the dump and refuse heaps excavated at the Fayum and Oxyrhynchus. As it was up until a few years ago in the Western world, literary men and those in the lowest economic class rarely came together. The affluent rubbed elbows frequently with men of letters, and writers sought out the affluent because they needed financial backing. Writers could not support themselves by writing only, a fact about which Martial and Juvenal complain so bitterly. There was no such thing as a copyright and consequently no royalties were paid. The relationships of writers and patrons made interesting marriages: patrons like Augustus wanted artists to portray their reigns in glowing words, while other patrons desired mere social prominence; authors needed the money.

The middle class in which centurions lived was able to, and apparently did, purchase books. And it is this middle-class audience to whom Chariton directed his novel. We might suggest that Chariton wrote what the middle class wanted to read, or even that his work struck a respondent chord in the middle class. Though Chariton writes about characters in the upper class who are above himself and his readers in station (Northrop Frye's "high mimetic" mode), in action and emotional development and discipline they are actors very much like the author and his reader (Frye's "low mimetic" mode). It is perhaps useful to note here the predilection of lower-class people to write about the upper classes and vice versa. Scholars have frequently commented on Petronius's preference to write about the lower classes. Surely this is merely the opposite side of the coin to Chariton's description of the nobility. Chariton does not, however, really paint the contemporary aristocracy; he simply projects his own middle-class views on members of the upper classes. Neither Chaereas, Callirhoe, nor the Persian nobility have the aristocratic bearing, despotic approach, or outrageous manners which came from centuries of ruling and occupying privileged positions in a structured and closed society. In Books 5 and 6 of Chariton's novel King Artaxerxes of Persia is not the Persian king but rather Chariton's projection of a middle-class Greek onto the Persian throne. The characters, both good and bad, have no real positive thrust toward good or evil. Virtue in the abstract is not a concern of Chariton or his audience; obedience to middle-class mores is the highest good. Virtue and heroism to Callirhoe mean protecting her sexual reputation; to Chaereas the heroic means not allowing himself to be made a cuckold, and in not allowing what is his to be taken from him. The outlook of both hero and heroine is passive; neither one is the dynamic hero of Greek epic or drama.

Much of the earlier Greek imaginative literature (all in the poetic medium, to be sure) was heroic, aristocratic, and concerned with the moral and ethical problems based on the nationalism of country, region, or city. This literature was to a large extent intellectual. But with the rise of prose fiction, and for us Chariton's romance in particular, we enter a literary creation built for the middle class by a middle-class writer. The literature here is not intellectual but sentimental. Indirectly, we are asked to suspend our intellectual and ethical powers and believe our author's simple approach to cosmic powers and to humanity. In this sentimental world the good as well as the bad are somehow inherently virtuous, and in the end an external force will sort out the black sheep from the white. With his ethical and intellectual defenses gone, the reader of a sentimental story lies open to attack from every emotion; actions in the sentimental romance elicit from the reader a flood of these emotions unhindered by reason. It is the desire and call for these romances from the middle class which encouraged Chariton to write. It is the middle class's lack of understanding of their cosmic existence which permitted Fortune to play such a large role in the action of Greek romances. Fortune separates the young lovers in the opening pages of the romance, keeps them apart throughout the whole work (and in so doing extends all the action in the romance), and finally reunites them.

III *The Rise of the Individual*

Though we have no intention, nor do we feel capable, of writing a sociological or psychological study of the individual in the ancient world, a word or two should be inserted here about the individual because it is pertinent to our study. The rise, i.e., the isolation from the group or clan, of the individual and the alienation of average people from the earlier all-encompassing city or city-state did not bring about the birth of fiction. Prose fiction was surely the brainchild of a literary mind and impulse. Alienation of the individual did, however, encourage the growth of prose fiction and gave it a fertile field in which to grow.

The social and civic surroundings that made epic and drama a literary expression of the soul of the city and of each of its citizens had been destroyed in the Hellenistic world that followed the death of Alexander the Great (323 B.C.). Drama and epic had been built on myths and heroes in myth, which on an archetypal level had struck a respondent chord in the souls of the Greeks. The original purposes for cities changed, some were destroyed, and people migrated from one place in the empire to another. The relevance and importance of the Greek city and, in fact, of being Greek finally passed out of existence under the Roman Empire, which stretched from sunrise to sunset. With it also went the relevance of man to the city-state. The Greek man was stripped of his old political alliances and also from his security, his points of reference. He became a man alone in the vast, impersonal Roman Empire, and before long he began to search for new security. He needed the kind of security that would not attach him to one place, a security he could carry with himself and so find a home anywhere in the empire. The hero—whether cultural, social, or political—to which he had earlier compared himself had become irrelevant in a world so big that heroes were outside the realm of credibility. Once external forces had done away with the city or city-state's independence, the individual found himself thrown back on his own emotional resources.

The new man could have adopted an existential view, but there seems to be no evidence that he did. Lost in this new and boundless world, some turned to mystery religions, some to hopeless atheism, some to the deity within themselves, and some to a personal identity in love. The characters in Chariton's novel (perhaps, in part, idealistic images of individual men in Aphrodisias) find identification in a religion with no national ties and in personal relationships of love which transcend any allegiance to birthplace or nationality. These characters live as individuals with little or no thought for their own society or kind. To have allegiance to a society and empire as big as that which the Romans had put together is to have no allegiance at all.

A second group of people find identification in a religious union within some mystery cult. This applies only in part to the characters in Chariton's work. The mystery religions came from the East and stood closed to all except the initiated or baptized; but once on the inside the participants had a sense of belonging to something. Though mystery cults had no national or political boundaries, to the lost and bewildered they offered a haven. The disenfranchised lower and middle classes found reality and a sense of direction within the closed mystery cult of the Christian community. There was work to do and all were asked to share the burdens. We witness here a new social accountability: lost individuals were fed, protected, and given responsibilities within the early church, i.e., the new society. Chaereas and Callirhoe, the protagonists in Chariton's novel, both belong to the *Society of Aphrodite*.

These are some of the ways in which individuals with no identity or sense of belonging tried to adapt themselves to a new situation. Many, however, could not or would not adjust, and we can detect a hopelessness and despair among certain classes of people which is unparalleled today except perhaps in urban and rural ghettos. Within these classes there existed a galloping pessimism that everything was in the hands of Fate (Tyche to the Greeks), who showed no particular concern for man, and that the situation was going from bad to worse. Franz Cumont, who has studied thoroughly the religious climate of the first-century A.D. Roman Empire, has graphically illustrated this pervasive pessimism: a reading of Greek and Latin epitaphs has focused attention on the high frequency of recurring themes, all illustrative of the belief that death is, in a real sense, a release from the tomb of the body (Orphism *sōma sēma*). One of the most interesting epitaphs and one which is found repeated again and again is:

NON FUI   FUI   NON SUM   NON CURO[8]
(I was not, I was, I am not, I do not care)

If we see fiction as the genre of the printed page, and epic and drama as the genres of the speaker and audience and actor and audience respectively, we can conclude that to a great extent epic and drama thrive in a society conscious of itself as a society and that fiction on the printed page fits well into an individualized society. Fiction could be read in isolation (whereas epic and drama insist on participation with the group) because it asked for no group activity; it created a fanciful world in which the reader could lose himself, and it illustrated the way in which a man beset with all kinds of troubles (like Chaereas) could persevere to a happy end.[9]

IV   *Limits of the Form*

Ancient rhetoricians themselves (see especially Macrobius, *Commentarii in Somnium Scipionis* I, 2, 6-12) divided prose narrative into two broad categories. The first has to do with plot and action and has three sections: *fabula, historia,* and *argumentum.* The Latin term *fabula* (Greek: *pseudēs historia* = *mythos*) is a type of narrative which is neither true nor does it approximate actual events. *Historia* (Greek: *alēthēs historia*) is an accurate record of the memory of what happened. The Latin word *argumentum* (Greek *hōs alēthēs historia* = *plasma*) signifies a story plot or imagined situation which could very easily have taken place. The second large category is concerned more with persons and less with events and plots, and leads to biography (i.e., biography mixed with drama) and narratives about individuals which deemphasize action.

Luckily for us Macrobius (ca. A.D. 400) commented further on the *fabula* and cited examples of what the ancients considered *fabulae* to be. *Fabulae* presented according to Macrobius two aspects, depending on their intent. Some *fabulae* were written merely to delight the listener (*delectatio*), while others were meant to edify or instruct the audience (*utilitas*). Since in antiquity it was felt that literature had to be useful for something, i.e., had to possess *ultilitas*, *fabulae* that were written for entertainment (*delectatio*) were considered nonserious examples of *fabulae.* Under *fabulae-delectatio* Macrobius subsumes the comedies of Menander and the *Satyricon* of Petronius, together with Apuleius's *Metamorphoses*; under *fabulae-utilitas* he places the fables of Aesop which are meant to educate and correct the listener.

With regard to overall plot, structure, and specific episode, the *Satyricon* of Petronius and the *Metamorphoses* of Apuleius are very close to *The Adventures of Chaereas and Callirhoe.* The so-called five Greek and three Latin romances form a closed society: they resemble each other in many ways and at the same time are very different from anything else in classical literature. We can feel reasonably safe if we state that classical critics probably would have analyzed Chariton's work as a *fabula-delectatio.* Macrobius says in addition that *fabulae* are similar to stories from tragedy, and Chariton himself refers to his own work as a drama.

The English word fable is too close etymologically to the Latin word *fabula* which renders the former word useless. Semantically, they differ too much for our purposes. Thus, because we cannot speak of Chariton's work as a fable, we propose to call it a novel or romance. In the recent literature of ancient prose fiction both terms, novel and romance, have been applied to works like Chariton's.[10] The word romance (French and German *roman*) comprises our usual use of the term novel and in addition includes other related types of extended prose narratives. We appreciate the careful distinctions that critics like Northrop Frye have erected between novel and romance, and these deserve preservation in theoretical critical works. But we have here the practical task of examining one work of art. To those who carefully observe the detailed terms of literary criticism, we would have to say that Chariton's work is indeed very close to Frye's definition of a romance.[11] Frye claims that the difference between the novel and the romance rests in the delineation of characters: the novelist portrays believable characters in a world of realism; the writer of romance sets out stylized creations, psychological archetypes from his actively subjective imagination. Novelists place characters with well-developed superegos (*persona*) within a defined and structured society. Romancers build figures who can move with greater freedom in time and space, unfettered by confining reality, dependent only on the talent and imagination of the writer.

Characters from romance are fanciful, but in their fancy often strike respondent chords in the daydreaming and fantasy of the reader. Whereas novels are built on plot, romances depend on motifs. And in these motifs lie the Jungian archetypes with which the readers consciously or unconsciously identify motifs in their own lives. Then too, it appears that readers throughout the ages have more warmly associated themselves with characters from romance who are involved in dreamlike affairs in imaginary settings than with characters from novels, whose developed personalities and superegos ward off much of human feeling.

But rarely is a piece of prose fiction pure novel or pure romance. There are usually enough realistic elements from the pure novel in each item of narrative prose fiction to make that item believable, and also enough ingredients from romance to make it subjectively relevant. The student (or critic) discusses at his peril the romance as a defective form of the novel or considers the romance a novel in its embryonic stage.

One of the severest criticisms of romance (as opposed to the novel) is that it is not realistic. We have been taught to think that the epithet "realistic" is an adjective of praise given by a critic to a good piece of literature. On closer examination the term realistic should be uncovered as a mere descriptive adjective of a type of literature, not a judgment on its worth. While James Joyce's *Ulysses* is not realistic, Philip Roth's *Portnoy's Complaint* might be. Realism here is hardly a criterion for good literature. Our obsession for, and striving after, realism in literature has been studied by Erich Auerbach in some detail in his influential book *Mimesis: The Representation of Reality in Western Literature.*[12] Auerbach's thesis is that the closer a literary work of art approximates real *mimesis,* the better it is as a work of art. Though Auerbach is a mighty critic, we believe that this line of reasoning in its extreme form is fallacious. In the complete abandonment of reality at various places in his work, Chariton seems to expect his audience to arrest its intellectual judgment and accept with an outpouring of emotion his sentimental situations and characters. Chariton tries to affect the emotions of his audience by portraying a heroine with an incredibly lofty level of morality who succeeds to happiness and all kinds of rewards because of her virtue. The outpouring of emotions from the heroine are expected to infect the audience and produce in return and in reaction an echo of sympathetic emotions. This sentimentality in Chariton seems foreign to many of us, jaded by generations of realistic writers who have shown us heroines with pimply faces and flat chests.

V   A Form About to Be

In our day the novel is so common and all-encompassing that it has through syncretism absorbed epic, satire, dialogues, tragedy-comedy, and parts of history. This development is recent and does not extend back in time to the ancient world, where the novel played a fairly small part in literature. The quality of the ancient novel, compared with contemporary products, is frequently disappointing, and the substance is found too often to be stereotyped. Furthermore, the ancient novel was written for a very narrow spectrum of the reading public. From its very humble origin the novel has reached outward to become all things to all people and upward to improve itself. But we must go back in time to that relatively dim past in the history of Greece, after the age of Homer when writing became an art, to seek the origins of the novel. It is the study of a literary form about to be.

The eight ancient novels that survive down to the present day represent that genre at its height and not at the early point to which we would like to direct our inquiries. These novels probably remind their readers not so much of contemporary novels as of current wide-screen movies, where episodes flash by in dizzying numbers, heroes perform incredible deeds, and heroines are rescued at the end of the last reel. Other modern readers will find these ancient novels modern in many ways, a fact which attests to their modernity at the time they were written. With respect to the action and method of rapidly changing scenes, many of the ancient novels resemble Fielding's *Tom Jones.*

In addition to appreciating any novel, it is in the nature of the human animal to try to learn where it came from. In this section of our discussion we will follow fairly carefully the aesthetic principle first applied to ancient prose fiction by Ben Perry,[13] who in turn had read and followed the advice of Croce and Hack,[14] that each literary product is to a greater or lesser extent a unique work of art, which nevertheless has many features in common with other works of art. The basic common denominator of any genre is the individual composition. Though its form is similar to other works, this does not necessarily restrict or define its content. An understanding of the elements and motifs of a work is not the same as an understanding of the work in its totality. Genre designation is at best a weak description to help the uninitiated grasp a work of art.

Since an ancient novel is a unique work of art, it stands in a real sense isolated. Other works, though not necessarily proto-novels, to which critics could apply descriptive terms similar to those they use for novels, may have influenced one novel or other and one writer or another, but they did not create the novel. The birth of the novel in antiquity was not owing to some

evolutionary force at work in literature, though the evolutionary explanation for the existence of anything is most attractive
and convincing in our age. Though the extant ancient novels
have many external similarities, each is a thing apart from the
others, unique, the creation by conscious effort of an artistic
drive. Many earlier genres, literary fashions, social and political
movements, political stresses of the age, and the force of contemporary artistic personalities, all contributed something to
the birth of the novel. The building materials were thus present;
the motivating impulse in the creator put them in order.

Nor was the ancient novel the misbegotten offspring or
transformation of some other genre. When epic no longer stood
as a viable art form, it did not survive under the guise of the
novel. When drama lost its city-state stage and the intellectual
stimuli necessary for survival, its remains were not rescued by
the novelists and reconstructed into a quasi-new form. But let us
again qualify this seemingly dogmatic statement: epic and
drama did make contributions and influence ancient prose
fiction, as did the social movements in the Mediterranean world
at this time. Each writer brought something unique to his work
and creatively borrowed other things from existing literary
fashions.

It is estimated that Homer lived and wrote the *Iliad* and
Odyssey around 800 B.C. In addition to these famous epics there
existed at about the same time an entire cycle of epics about
many local heroes of various Greek lands. The only other
complete, extant, ancient Greek epic is Apollonius of Rhodes's
(b. 295 B.C.) *Argonautica*. According to Jaroslav Ludvikovsky,[15]
the ancient novel arose or was created from the remnants of
the defunct epic and bankrupt historiography. In a real sense
this is to say nothing. One genre does not die and then by itself
arise as something else—unless a force or idea within a writer
makes it happen. When a writer or group of writers create a new
genre, they do not adopt and repair an old genre and call it
their own form. Epic is born and dies because it has lost its
purpose for existence; a new form, whatever it is, has also a
new purpose for being. The ancient novel surely borrowed from
epic (and borrowed heavily) but arose to fulfill a new need,
to satisfy a new kind of writer, and to fill a vacuum left in

literary forms. The novel, for instance, borrowed some of the character types, descriptions of battles, and a peculiar outlook toward the hero and heroine. Had any contemporary critic praised Chariton for originating a new form in the novel, Chariton would have been surprised and offended.

Chariton and all ancient writers were tied closely to tradition, and the highest form of praise would have been a compliment on how well he performed within the tradition. Ancient writers preferred creative borrowing to originality; Vergil's use of Homer is a good example. To both Greeks and Romans there is a vast difference between creative borrowing, i.e., one genre from another, and the development of a genre. The creation of the novel is the creation by an artist who consciously and primarily intends to write a novel or something very much like it, and secondarily borrows trappings from other forms of literature. We do not believe that the novel developed by steps like a biological organism. Writers as literary opportunists set down words in certain arrangements, of infinite variety, and without regard to a superimposed law of order. Plants develop in complete separation from the will of man, often growing best when man never interferes. The novel arises only when and where men will it.

VI *The Influence of Epic*

Epic had general influences on all the later forms of literature in the Graeco-Roman world, and survives as the oldest literary genre from antiquity. The greatest epic writer was Homer, and though dead for nine hundred years when Chariton and others wrote their novels, he cast a long shadow over the new genre. In the influence of the epic it is not so much the force of the *Iliad* as that of the *Odyssey*, for in the latter we find all the elements necessary for a successful novel: the marvelous, the erotic, and the violent. The *Iliad*, with its carefully delineated Greek-style hero, lacks the cosmopolitan appeal of the marvelous *Odyssey* with its adventurous and wandering hero. The *Iliad* describes a Greek world with Greek interests, morality, and standard of values; it belongs body and soul to the closed society of eighth-century B.C. Greece.

The tone and feeling in the *Odyssey* is different; it casts aside nationality and presents a cosmopolitan hero, a man at home in any place. The world of the *Odyssey* is a world of interest to all men. The travels of Odysseus (like the travels in *2001: A Space Odyssey*) take him to all reaches of the known world, exploring exotic and fairy-tale places, tumbling with incredibly beautiful women, and defeating monstrous foes. The embryonic novel to a large extent already resides in the *Odyssey*. A failure of the ancient heroic will encouraged a change in the epic form and so opened the way for the novel.

Our interest here is not in the epic itself, but in its death. In their indispensable study, *The Nature of Narrative*,[16] Scholes and Kellogg look at the breakup of the Greek epic and the resultant influence on the ancient novel. These two scholars see in the epic a synthesis of elements which, destroyed, yields two antithetical kinds of narrative, the fictional and the empirical. When epic storytellers are no longer interested in the "traditional story" or the *mythos* but are concerned more with entertainment (fiction) or truth (history), they cease to produce epics, and the form dies. According to the scheme of Scholes and Kellogg, as the empirical (real) narrative emerges from the epic synthesis it assumes two forms: the historical and the mimetic; as the fictional (ideal) emerges it takes two forms: the romantic and the didactic (fables). The ideal (fictional) part of the epic synthesis is the part that concerns us in our study. The writer, like Chariton, of ideal narratives breaks first with traditional stories (epic) and then sets his writing (the ideal) in opposition to the empirical (the real, history). His search for "truth" takes him along artistic roads not scientific, and his world is ruled by poetic and artistic justice, not the cold reality of law and cosmic order. The intent of the writer of fiction is to delight (romance) or edify (fable).

After the *Iliad* and *Odyssey* it is obvious that epic became more literary and fictional and less dependent on traditional stories. In Apollonius's *Argonautica* (ca. 250 B.C.) and Vergil's *Aeneid* (19 B.C.), we can observe a significant shift from strict observation of recreating the traditional story (primary epic) toward creation of pure fiction (Greek romance).

Our task at this point is to isolate, if possible, those influences, or more exactly apparent influences, of the epic and its tradition on the written ancient romance. Before Homer's age people had gathered to hear wandering storytellers relate incredible adventures. Homer earned his living in that fashion, and we learn from Quintilian[17] and others that in the first-century A.D. Roman Empire *fabulatores* worked a regular circuit, telling stories of all kinds to people too poor to purchase books. To the man who could afford one-tenth of a denarius the storyteller would unfold his *fabula*.[18]

Epic and prose narratives have much in common by way of presentation. In epic we have a visible storyteller with a tale confronting a visible audience; in prose fiction we also have a teller of a tale meeting an audience. But in the words of Northrop Frye the "radical of presentation" is changed, though the genre of epic is very similar to that of fiction. The radical of presentation of the epic is the "spoken word and listener." When this epic is written down and given out on a printed page, the spoken word, the speaker, and the audience have all become hypothetical; the radical of presentation is changed to the printed page and yields fiction. When the audience no longer appreciates or desires to work with poetry, the fictional thesis of the epic synthesis is set down in prose, and we see a new kind of literature, indistinguishable from prose fiction.[19]

Perhaps the greatest contribution of the epic to later prose fiction was the motivational device of the journey. Frye says that "of all fictions, the marvelous journey is the one formula that is never exhausted."[20] In the third-millennium B.C. Assyrian epic, which is called simply the *Epic of Gilgamesh*, we already see the marvelous journey of the hero Gilgamesh, searching for life. A better known epic and one which strongly influenced Chariton was the *Odyssey*, in which the hero made a long journey in search of his homeland. The bulk of the *Odyssey* concerned the adventures of this journey, with only a small section at the conclusion for the reunion of Odysseus and his wife Penelope. Chariton imitated (consciously and in order to connect his work with the famous epic) this same general outline, including a similar search motif for the wife and the marvelous journey. Whereas Homer arranged to have love affairs for Odysseus while Penelope remained faithful at home, Chariton decided that romantic interludes should fall to Callirhoe separated from Chaereas. Homer's audience expected twelfth-century B.C. heroes to act like despots, high-handedly, and only out of concern for their reputations. Chariton's characters were expected to conform to popular middle-class morality and to act the part of a young married couple. Two elements that dominate in the *Odyssey,* travel and love, also played major roles in Chariton's novel.

It is worthwhile to mention again that Chariton had no real intention to write an epic in prose. But because epic, unlike its role in our own culture, was so visible to literary society, Chariton tried by imitation and parody to echo elements of epic. One parallel Chariton constructed between epic and his novel was oral recitation. The *Odyssey* was meant to be memorized and then spoken aloud by a traveling singer. Traces of oral narrative in Homer's works have been illustrated and documented by many scholars.[21] Traces of oral narrative and technique have also been found in *The Adventures of Chaereas and Callirhoe*, where Chariton could have only consciously put them in to imitate Homer. Chariton intended obviously that his audience should make the connection between his novel and Homer's epics.[22]

Another epic convention which Chariton imitated was the use of *formulae. Formulae* are short or long units which an oral storyteller uses again and again as he constructs his poem. By stringing these *formulae* together in different ways a storyteller can build large sections of his poem with familiar (and somewhat repetitious) material. If a reciter is going to tell from memory twenty thousand lines of an epic, the use of *formulae* would be a very successful device to aid his memory. Again, though he did not need *formulae* in written prose fiction, Chariton frequently resorted to their use. Another epic convention followed by Chariton was that of summarizing. Chariton acted as if the reader had no text to consult or look back at to check what happened in earlier episodes, and so summarized in full at three places the previous events. This was a necessary device for oral narrative but hardly for the written word. Then, as if these references to epic were not enough, Chariton directly quoted Homer in his peculiar dialect more than twenty times.

VII *The Influence of Drama*

Like epic, drama influenced the ancient novel both by its vitality and also by its death. The removal of drama (both tragedy and comedy) from public functions in the face of more spectacular (and less demanding intellectually) events, or because it served best and only a small, closed society of people who could relate to its deeper meanings, created a vacuum into which the novel moved. The incredibly large number of theatres scattered around the Greek and Roman world (every self-respecting town had at least one theatre) is a false indication and measurement of the vitality of their theatre life. Theatre buildings were used for all kinds of things, mimes, recitation, poetry readings (Nero for example), and worse— athletic events of the lowest kinds.

The influence of drama on Chariton is as telling as that of epic. At one point in *The Adventures of Chaereas and Callirhoe* Chariton describes the troubles Chaereas has to endure as part of the melancholy *drama* staged by Fortune (Bk. 4, Chap. 4). And then after Chariton had set before his audience a tense courtroom scene, he asks the reader:

What playwright ever staged such a drama? You, reader, probably thought you were in a theatre confronting actors and sharing with them their weeping and joy, amazement and pity, shock and anger. (Bk. 5, Chap. 8)

Heliodorus and Achilles Tatius also refer to their works as dramas.[23]

The sentimentality of the action and the idealism of the characters in many of the ancient novels indicate an appeal to the reading middle classes whose values were different from the earlier theatre-going upper classes. In a way, we can refer to ancient prose fiction as melodrama. The good and bad are separated, easily recognizable, and conspicuous. The hero personifies virtue, and the villain exists merely to torture the hero. The conflict of good and evil is black and white, and clear to anyone who cares to see. Because there is no grand cosmic design to the melodramatic world, and because the conflicts of hero and villain are never inevitable but only chance happenings, and because salvation or death, happiness or sorrow are sudden, gratuitous, or two minutes too late, the ancient novels are seldom restful, quiet, restrained, or simple. This is very unlike the Greek tragic drama which the Greek novelists wished to imitate. As the modern French playwright Anouilh says in his play *Antigone*:

In a Greek tragedy nothing is in doubt and everyone's destiny is known. That makes for tranquility. There is a sort of fellow feeling among characters in a tragedy: he who kills is as innocent as he who gets killed: it's all a matter of what part you are playing. Tragedy is restful; and the reason is that hope, that foul, deceitful thing, has no part in it.

Each person in attendance at a Greek tragedy knew the plot and outcome of each play; accordingly the playwright in good classical tradition stressed form. Though emphasizing different elements and intended for different audiences, drama and the novel in antiquity did, nevertheless, have much in common. In drama it was the accepted practice that a playwright invent some of the action and some of the characters (fiction); drama is the first genre of imaginative literature in Greece. When drama faded away and at the same time a reading public arose, the freedom of pure invention passed from drama to the novel. As concerns major literary products in antiquity, only drama and the novel were acceptable forms for *concentrated* fiction; historiography permitted short fictional segments.

Early classical tragedy, which was part of the religious tradition of the Greeks, was based largely on myth with some invention left to the author, especially in the roles and speeches of messengers and in other minor characters. From its very beginning (based on extant examples) comedy was always clearly and totally fiction. Then toward the end of Euripides's life (d. 406 B.C.) invention on the part of the tragic playwright grew as the subject matter switched to lesser known myths and legends, which by their very nature gave more freedom to the imagination. A fine example of this in later

Greek drama is Euripides's *Electra*, which rests on a variant Greek myth. In it this last of the three great Greek tragedians invented freely new episodes and changed the traditional descriptions of the characters. And, as it turns out, it is no tragedy at all, but rather a kind of comedy—an example of the so-called Middle Comedy. It is not a cosmic tragedy like *Oedipus Rex*, but rather a serious and psychological look at men's home on earth. And it is, to the horror of many, sentimental and emotional at times, with a simplified view of reality in which the human state is virtuous and that fine Greek intellectual bearing held in suspension. Electra's struggle is not with cosmic forces but with her frightened mother, hesitant brother, and with a simple goatherd, whom she was forced to marry. She is not wrestling with fate but rather searching for personal identity and, as an important afterthought, protecting with the help of her goatherd husband her maidenhead. This identical and improbable scene is repeated in Xenophon of Ephesus's *Anthia and Habrocomes* (Bk. 2, Chap. 8ff.). Chariton proposes a similar situation (Bk. 2) when Dionysius marries Callirhoe, who is still married to Chaereas and carrying his baby. But Chariton does not expect his audience to believe that Callirhoe can protect her "virtue" in the face of such force. Callirhoe gives in to an impossible situation, and Chariton develops a more realistic situation than Euripides.

It is the free invention plus the serious and sentimental tone that later writers of Greek Middle Comedy (a form of drama known as comedy because of its happy endings) adopted, and which passed then to ancient romance. The outward form of drama passed into obscurity; its content was assumed by the novel; and its audience became readers of fiction. The form of tragedy was tightly knit, while that of comedy was episodic, and as tragedy developed (or broke up, if that is a better epithet) and as it grew closer to comedy, it also became more episodic until New Comedy (a type of comedy which spun off from Euripidean Middle Comedy and not from the Old Comedy of Aristophanes) was nothing if it was not episodic. The dramatists' freedom of invention, of course, hastened the process of piling episode on episode. Thus the writers of the ancient novel: they had the freedom to invent their own stories and quickly used (like Chariton) or misused (like Achilles Tatius and Heliodorus) this opportunity to compose episodes. The sentimental tone and happy endings of later drama (Middle and New Comedy) were also adopted in varying degrees by the Greek novelists.

Perry is surely right when he says that Greek romance had an "elastic framework."[24] Modeled on Greek drama, many novels were merely extensions of the acts in a play. The novelist added or multiplied scenes, and stopped after a decent length, rather than after having completed a unified whole. Chariton, the closest to the dramatist in time and the earliest of the novelists, held (to his greater fame) the number of episodes to a respectable limit and generally succeeded in making them integral parts of the whole. As a rule each episode in Chariton, as in classical drama, was necessary for the progress of the story plot. The progress of action was motivated by causes within the story. Extraneous events, Lady Luck, Fortune, and *deus ex machina* were very infrequent. In some of the novels which followed Chariton's in succeeding centuries, the structure was almost totally episodic, and virtually all movement in the plot was caused by chance happenings barely related to the main thread of the story. Also, in later novels the reader can with cause suspect that some were written not for the narrative but as an excuse for a display of virtuosity and rhetoric.

Since 1906 scholars have recognized the close structural dependence of Chariton on drama, and Reitzenstein followed by Perry[25] has seen in *The Adventures of Chaereas and Callirhoe* the overall unity of a drama in five acts:

Act I	Books 1 - 3.2
II	3.3 - 4
III	5 - 6
IV	7
V	8

Within this structure there was only one climax (end of Bk. 8) with a steady progression toward it and only a short summary after it.

The position of the chorus in Greek drama was so important and its role so large that it was surely a distinguishing characteristic of the genre. Choruses do not now and have never belonged to the novel. But Chariton managed to find a place for it: for the chorus of drama Chariton substituted the assembled common people of the city. The function of a dramatic chorus was to set the mood, summarize the sentiments of opposing sides, plead for a common cause of goodness, and give, in a way, the spectators's reaction to the action of the drama. A good illustration of these functions of the chorus put to use by Chariton in the new role of the assembled people was the opening scene of the book, where Callirhoe's father, Hermocrates, reluctantly granted his daughter permission to marry Chaereas, his opponent's son. Because such a marriage alliance would be advantageous for the participants, their families, and the city in general, the assembled people spontaneously gathered in a special session and pleaded with Hermocrates to permit and bless the marriage. The crowd of assembled citizens of Syracuse here functioned as the chorus would have in ancient tragedy: the crowd knew (as did the author and readers) all the causes and consequences of the actions of the characters or actors, and the reader could appreciate the irony which arose from the disparity of understanding among the principals involved.[26]

Later Greek drama, including some of the last plays of Euripides, resolved its plots with recognition scenes rather than *deus ex machina* miracles; this became one of the set pieces in New Comedy. The denouement of *The Adventures of Chaereas and Callirhoe* was likewise a recognition scene and was structurally natural because the lovers had earlier been forcibly separated. The recognition scenes of Odysseus with his father, nurse, and dog in *Odyssey* 23 were of a special kind, for his appearance had been expected daily; his changed physical condition (after twenty years) alone made recognition scenes necessary. The happy ending of the *Odyssey*, as well as those of later Greek tragedy and those of New Comedy, which usually resulted from a previous recognition scene, were repeated by Chariton in Book 8 when Chaereas and Callirhoe recognized each other and returned home to live together happily ever after.

The influence of drama on ancient romance and in particular

on Chariton is surely obvious. Chariton in fact apparently is very eager to draw parallels and make connections between drama and his prose fiction. On at least two occasions (see above) he says he is telling a story which belongs in the theatre. Then, in the final scene in the novel, Chariton has Chaereas relate the whole story of events from beginning to end, what had happened to him and Callirhoe, to the citizens of Syracuse assembled in the *theatre*. The final impression Chariton wants to leave with his readers is that they have just witnessed a prose narrative which belongs in the theatre.

VIII *The Influence of Historiography*

While some scholars (notably Perry) maintain that written history had little or no influence on the novel, the opposition, made up of two factions, contends that it did have significant influence. The first of these factions holds that the novel, through an evolutionary process involving historiography, is a product of a national yearning for self-expression and a reaction against national frustrations. Conquered peoples create national heroic myths not necessarily for foreign propaganda but to bolster their pride in themselves and their past. A simple version of the theory is this: the legend of some early hero is expanded, other legends of similar heroes are grafted on to this, the material is subjected to certain literary forces and influences, and the resultant product envolves into a romance. An example of this type of historical-literary product is *The Romance of Alexander* by Pseudo-Callisthenes, a contemporary of Alexander the Great. The German scholar Martin Braun[27] has argued powerfully that the Egyptians, subdued and then incorporated into the empire of Alexander the Great, accepted or rationalized that Alexander was the son of Nectanebus, the last native Egyptian Pharaoh, and that, having created a romance around Nectanebus, replaced him with the greater hero Alexander. The legend of Alexander is thus credited with crowding out that of Nectanebus. Braun contends that a history of Alexander written during his life or shortly thereafter did not degenerate into *The Romance of Alexander*. Rather it was the other way around. The legend of Alexander was very

popular in such Eastern Hellenized cities as Alexandria, where
the Greek and Egyptian races mingled easily, and from there
under the influence of historiography was written down in a
form that imitated history. From its beginning as legend it rose
to the level of uncritical history and thence to romance. Since
much of ancient history was uncritical, the legend and romance
of Alexander was taken for history. This theory is all the more
acceptable if Braun is right when he says that the legend grew
up around, and belonged spiritually and socially to, the common
people, who did not differentiate between history in the
written form and literary fiction.

Another interesting work in this no-man's-land of genre,
fragments of which were found in 1893, is the so-called *Ninus
Romance*. Braun feels that this work, like *The Romance of
Alexander*, arose from popular, middle-class legend, until it
approached the underside of respectable history. Ninus, the
hero of the romance and eponymous founder of Assyrian
Nineveh, marries Semiramis, queen of Babylon. This romance
differs from that of Alexander because in *Ninus Romance* we
find a real element of erotic action and reaction. To the erotic
ingredient is added that of travel to far-off lands. The Assyrians
and Babylonians both fell under the heel of the conquering
Persians, and, losing their earlier antagonism for each other,
appreciated a common fate. As an expression of their frustration
and at the same time a desire to keep current the past glorious
days of Assyria and Babylon, the *Ninus Romance* was created.
The legend, repeated often enough, approached the realm of
history. The level of love and travel ingredients, while only in
part enhancing the character of the hero and heroine, do reflect
the middle-class milieu from which it sprang.

A scholar holding a slightly different view from the first
faction is John Barnes, who believes that the Greek romance
developed from historiography, but in Egypt rather than in
Greece.[28] He works through papyri whose stories go back into
the third millennium B.C. and concern adventures of sailors
traveling to exotic lands and undergoing fantastic risks. A papyrus of 1300 B.C. entitled the *Doomed Prince* tells how a prince
obtains by contest the king's daughter, though the king is un-
willing, and later how she helps him in his dangerous adven-

tures. This type of quasi-historical romance continues in Egypt at least to the second century B.C., from where we have received the *Dream of Nectanebus*. As pointed out earlier, Nectanebus is connected to *The Romance of Alexander*. The hero of the *Dream of Nectanebus* is named Petesis, and the papyrus breaks off just at the point where he finds the most beautiful girl in the world. The story has elements both of love and of travel-adventure. But about this romance we have one other vital piece of information: it was translated from the demotic Egyptian into Greek! In this lies a connection between the Egyptian romances and the as yet unborn Greek romances. Barnes is of the opinion that Greek romance is not an indigenous form, but rather an importation from Egypt where it had existed for three thousand years before one example was translated into Greek. As further evidence for Egyptian influence, we can note that Egypt is at the center of the romance world, and that all Greek romances (except *Daphnis and Chloe*) have episodes in Egypt. Barnes, agreeing in part with Braun, holds that some of the "Greek" romances were probably written primarily for a Greek reading public in Egypt. The present reader will want to recall that the Ptolemy pharoahs of Egypt were Greek and not Egyptian and that Alexandria was a Greek city.

Those who hold to the theory that the origin of Greek romance rests on the influence of historiography never fail to mention that the historian Xenophon of Athens (ca. 430-360 B.C.) wrote something very similar to a romance in his *Cyropaedia* (*Education of Cyrus*), an idealized and fictional biography of the growth and journey through life of Cyrus, prince of Persia. In addition to a careful and romantic description of the idealized hero, Cyrus, we find here many of the narrative elements of travel-adventure and love. The love story of Abradates and his faithful wife Panthia, and the chivalrous action of Araspas in removing himself before a love-triangle develops, can rank with scenes from most romances. Besides those famous historians Herodotus and Thucydides, the Greeks produced a raft of second, third, and lesser rated historians (Ctesias, for example), who altered historiography from a reporting of the factual to a dramatic presentation of the interesting, marvelous, strange, exotic, and paradoxical. We can see a foreshadowing of this already in the above-mentioned *Cyropaedia*. Though Ctesias (fl. 400 B.C.) may not be the father of "tragic history," he is one of its earliest and most influential practitioners. In his *History of Persia* and *History of India*[29] we can see that he is not at all interested in history itself but merely in recording strange and unexplainable events (births of monsters, for example), which are intended to stir the emotions rather than the contemplative senses of the reader. Some stories are meant to shock. Then, because he doubts the audience will believe such tales, Ctesias swears that he saw with his own eyes everything he reports.

Tragic history became very popular in the Hellenistic Age (that amorphous age after the death of Alexander in 323 B.C.) and for a time even supplanted the scientific reporting of events. Contemporary scholars refer to this kind of history as "tragic" because it shares so many characteristics with tragedy. Like tragedians, the intent of these historians was to arouse pity and fear and to thrill readers instead of reporting facts.[30] Tragic history can properly be seen as a mixture of two distinct genres —drama and history. Had Ctesias in his works adopted a structure with a unifying plot, we could have classified them as historical novels.

Such a mixture was apparently highly unstable and in time broke down and returned to its constituent parts. At least as early as the time of Aristotle it had been established as an aesthetic principle that the function of the poet and dramatist was to write fiction (what might happen) and the function of a historian was to set down real events in a real world (*Poetics* 9 and 24). Before the breakup of tragic history occurred, however, the influence of the form spread far and wide, more among the less discriminating than among the literary sophisticates.

One area ready-made for highbred tragic history was historial monographs. These biographies were ostensibly historical, but often (at the request of the principal figure) they were altered to allow room for fictional scenes and episodes of dramatic importance. In content and structure these monographs came very close to contemporary historical romances, for they displayed a kind of built-in plot and controlling unity: each monograph concerned itself with the life, growth, maturity, and rise to power and success of one man only. The unity derived from one central figure was enough to hold the work together. By chance we have a very personal and pertinent piece of information which can shed light on the nature of tragic history and historical monographs from a firsthand source. In a letter (*Familiares* 5.12) dated 56 B.C., Cicero asked the historian Lucceius to drop all his other work and write a monograph on Cicero's heroic actions in public life. This should not, however, be just an ordinary history; Lucceius was asked to embellish the bare facts with the kind of descriptions and anecdotes that belonged to drama and stirred the reader's emotions! Cicero was commissioning his own personal tragic history with himself at center stage.

In the hands of such men as Lucceius the vehicle of history carried as freight prose drama and narrative, designed to shock and amaze. It was perhaps not too long before storytellers recognized the new opportunity and, reversing the roles, wrote fiction disguised as history. This is the theory subscribed to by the second of the two factions introduced at the beginning of this section. Near this point in the life of tragic history, when fiction dominated historical reporting and drama set the tone of the work, it seems to have had its strongest effect on the ancient Greek novel. Literary men, opportunistic as any group of people, turned the tables on the historians who wrote history as drama and began to write drama as history. Chariton was the earliest extant Greek novelist, and he showed the influence of historiography more than later novelists, who developed the genre along novelistic rather than historiographical lines. Chariton set his novel in a definite period of time, in a definite location, and populated it with historical characters. But as others in later years developed the novel, they dropped the historical framework and relied on pure invention.

Reasons why Chariton adopted the historical form he did are probably not hard to find. Judging by his novel we can say that he was a literary conservative, not eager to throw over the traces of established traditions. Unbridled prose fiction had not been sanctioned by the literary establishment, but prose fiction disguised as history (or vice versa) could rest on the authority of "the ancients," Xenophon, Ctesias, Cicero. While history was

a form established by time and precedent, the novel was an
upstart, the kind of thing frowned upon among literary men.
But if a disguise, such as history, could be found, ancient critics
could rationalize that existence. We must remember that the
ancients, especially the intellectuals of the Roman empire, had
a marvelous capacity to rationalize, disguise, and hide reality
under other names.[31]

IX *Influence of the Love-Elegy*

The last (only in this schematic outline) identifiable literary
influence on the ancient novel is the Alexandrian love-elegy.
It is in some ways the most attractive account for the origin
of the ancient novel, especially as articulated by Giuseppe
Giangrande.[32] He, among others, has assigned history, including
tragic history to a minor role in the development of the novel.
In addition, he does not consider travel-adventure episodes or
plots built on the formula of a marvelous journey to be major
influences. Giangrande and certain European scholars hold that
the origin of the Greek romance goes back to Alexandrian love-
elegy, the type of elegy which sprang up in the Greek city of
Alexandria in Egypt around such figures as Callimachus (d.
240 B.C.). Giangrande sets aside all other influences on the
ancient novels and contends that each novel is based on, or
has its content involved in, the erotic:

The Leitmotif, the essential nucleus of the romance, is the story
of two lovers, be it diluted and lengthened by means of adventurous accretions.[33]

In his view the erotic is the efficient motif, driving the plot of
of the story on to its final denouement.

The Greek novel is not a history, an adventure story, or a
Reiseroman; it is a love story. But how are the many and persistent historical elements in the novels accounted for? Critics
proposing the love-elegy theory point out that Alexandrian
elegists used local legends, sagas, obscure myths, and regional
histories as "copy" for their poems. When love-elegies were
expanded and taken over by novelists, the strong historical
flavor remained in them.

Setting aside the influence of historiography, Giangrande deftly untangles the theory problem of how *prose* romance evolved from *poetic* love-elegy, and how sad love-elegies could produce optimistic novels. Elegies of love frequently conclude with tragic endings, an unthinkable denouement for a Greek novel. Many fine elegies, however, like Callimachus's *Acontius and Cydippe* have comic endings, and, it is surmised, later novelists borrowing from elegy obviously chose to ignore those elegies with sad endings. After falling in love at first sight, Acontius is separated from Cydippe who falls seriously ill under the influence of Artemis (because she refuses to marry Acontius). The elements of love at first sight, separation, and love-sickness close to death, are all incidents in Chariton's *The Adventures of Chaereas and Callirhoe.* Furthermore, Acontius and Chaereas must travel about before being united or reunited with their lovers.

While no single Alexandrian love-elegy contains all the ingredients (motifs) that it takes to make up a complete Greek novel, there has survived from antiquity a work called *Erotica Pathemata* (*Love Romances*) from the pen of one Parthenius (first century B.C.). The *Erotica Pathemata* is a collection of mythological tales written for the elegiac poet Gallus as a source book for his future poems. It is important to note that it was not composed for a mythographer or historian. The subject of these myths is passionate love and hate. "Take away the strictly mythological element (substitute, that is, the names of unknown persons for the semihistorical characters of whom the stories are related), and almost all might serve as the plots of novels."[34] Subsumed under the all-embracing efficient motif of love in the *Erotica Pathemata* are motifs of pirates, bandits, oracles, wars, marvelous rescues, and parental oppositions to marriages. Parthenius provided for Gallus a veritable motif gold mine.

One important problem remains: how did the poetry of love-elegy change into the prose of romance? Giangrande again provides a plausible solution. Because rhetoric and rhetorical training held the most important position in all scholastic training in the classical world, a dear price was placed on style in writing. An important exercise in rhetoric was the preparation of prose paraphrases of myths, stories, and even books of Homer. From Greek papyri found in Egypt we learn that such paraphrases were written before the first century B.C., or before the advent of the first novel. In addition to prose paraphrases by students, teachers, also, quite often composed them as examples or paradigms for students. As the students developed facility in prose, they began to write longer and longer compositions, and Giangrande has discovered among these certain ones written on the subject of erotic love. With this discovery he feels confident enough to claim, unequivocally, that Greek (love) romance originated with the prose paraphrases of Alexandrian love-elegies.

Though we have covered, at least cursorily, the generally accepted theories on the origin of the Greek novel, there is one more theory (not quite born yet, but its author is obviously pregnant with it) which we should mention. In a work of penetrating scholarship Sophie Trenkner[35] has argued that in popular oral literature, going back as early as the sixth century B.C., there were tales of adventure and love closely resembling later erotic Greek novels. These tales were popular first in Ionia (Greek settlements in Asia Minor) and with her writers—Herodotus, for example, set many popular short stories into the narrative of his history—and occur with astounding frequency in the later plays of Euripides and New Comedy. These tales, once New Comedy was no longer operant, became the novels we are now considering.

This apparently appealing theory does not concern itself with forms or genres but rather with varieties or kinds of literary motifs. Trenkner has not traced the development or origin of the novel form; her research has been limited to following motifs of love, adventure, and the marvelous, and documenting their survival in ancient novels. Hers is a masterful discussion of the parts, not of the whole. We must add, however, that like the love-elegy theory, it is in a way most attractive. Someone must raise it above its present status as a mere motif index, if we are ever to take it seriously.

X Conclusion

The reader has been given in the preceding pages a wide array of scholarly opinion, research, and results. Until we learn more from ancient sources, the origins of the Greek novel will reside under a certain amount of shade and stay hidden from our view. It is hoped that this discussion with its seemingly contradictory views will not lead the reader to despair of the study on one hand, or to think the present writers indecisive or lacking in conviction. A study of the subject matter for some years has taught us to beware of dogmatic statements and omniscient certainty. The reader is presented with a mere over-view of the modern thought on the subject and hopefully in the future he will be able to uncover more evidence, to perceive more clearly where we have walked in shadows, and finally to advance the study of ancient fiction to the point where there will be only one theory of the origin of Greek novels.

CHAPTER 3

Overview

I   The Adventures of Chaereas and Callirhoe

CHARITON'S novel is divided into eight books and presents itself to the reader in a straightforward plot line. The only possible confusion permitted the present generation of readers is difficulty with and remembering the names. To the reader unaccustomed to long Greek names or to the reader who cannot understand the root meanings of Greek names, the names in Chariton pose a possible problem. But nothing like the names in Tolstoy or Dostoevski. In our overview we will organize the material in each book under broad generic rubrics, providing the reader with a quick survey of the subject of each book.

Book 1.   *Religious Motifs + Marriage and Adultery +*
Pirate Adventures.

An incredibly handsome young boy, Chaereas, and girl, Callirhoe, meet at a religious festival of Aphrodite in Syracuse, fall in love and marry, though their fathers are bitter, political enemies. Disappointed suitors for the hand of Callirhoe accuse her of unfaithfulness and stir up the latent jealousy of Chaereas. In a rage Chaereas kicks Callirhoe who apparently dies; Callirhoe is buried and her husband threatens suicide. Theron, a daring pirate, robs Callirhoe's tomb and its riches, and, finding her alive, takes her along to be sold as a slave. Landing at Miletus in Asia Minor, Theron sells Callirhoe to a man named Leonas, chief steward to Dionysius, governor of Miletus, and encourages him to believe that Callirhoe could act as a kind of substitute for Dionysius's recently dead wife.

Book 2.   *Pure Romance + Motifs of New Comedy.*

In the temple of Aphrodite on his estate outside Miletus, Dionysius first meets and falls in love with Callirhoe, who is put in the hands of Phocas, chief overseer under Leonas, and his wife Plangon. Leonas tries in many ways (some not legal) to convince Callirhoe to love Dionysius. The net result for Leonas would be the undying gratitude and munificence of Dionysius. Plangon is playing the same game as Leonas, but with better results. Her goal is freedom from slavery for her husband and herself. Both Leonas and Plangon are types of mischievous characters from New Comedy. In the bath Plangon observes that Callirhoe is pregnant with Chaereas's child (Dionysius knows nothing of Chaereas) and persuades her to marry Dionysius and trick him into believing the child is his.

Book 3. *Without Benefit of Clergy: End of Act I +* *Chaereas to the Rescue Almost.*

Dionysius and Callirhoe are married in Miletus with great pomp and parade. Chariton now switches the scene of action from Miletus back to Syracuse, where we find Chaereas standing at Callirhoe's empty tomb. Here begins Act II of this drama. Chaereas and the relatives of Callirhoe soon discern the actions of the tomb robbers and set sail to track them down. As it happens, Chaereas comes upon the ship of Theron, who claims he is merely a passenger on the ill-fated derelict vessel. Through various tortures Theron tells the whole story of the tomb robbery and sale of Callirhoe in Miletus. He is impaled forthwith, and Chaereas sets out for Miletus. Phocas learns of Chaereas's presence near Miletus, and, realizing the imminent destruction of his enchanted master, has local barbarians attack Chaereas's ship. Chaereas escapes death and is sold into slavery to Mithridates, governor of Caria, a province of the Persian Empire in southwest Asia Minor. Dionysius learns of Chaereas's existence only after his (he never learned the truth) son was born. Acting out of jealousy he has Phocas inform Callirhoe that Chaereas died accidentally when attacked by brigands.

Book 4. *Confusion + Chaos + Comic Complexity.*

To seal the death of Chaereas in Callirhoe's mind Dionysius erects a large tomb for Chaereas and holds a magnificent funeral to which he invites Mithridates, governor of Caria, and Pharnaces, governor of Lydia (a neighboring province), both of whom fall in love with Callirhoe. Back in Caria, Chaereas, an innocent bystander to a slave revolt, is about to be crucified when he is rescued by Mithridates in the hope that through him he can acquire Callirhoe. Mithridates convinces Chaereas to write a letter to Callirhoe, who Chaereas knows is now alive, and tell her he also is alive. This letter falls into the hands of Dionysius, who is terrified to learn that Chaereas might be alive but who, on closer inspection, suspects that Mithridates sent the letter to get Callirhoe for himself. Without hesitation Dionysius appeals to Pharnaces, his immediate superior and governor of Lydia and Ionia, to have Mithridates prosecuted. Pharnaces, hoping to get Callirhoe, appeals to Artaxerxes, King of Persia and Asia Minor, to give Dionysius satisfaction. Artaxerxes also is in love with Callirhoe, if only by rumor, and orders all parties to his capital. End of Act II.

Book 5. *Callirhoe's Ordeal* + *Trial by Jury*.

Mithridates arrives in Babylon first but is forced to await Dionysius's presence. The women of Babylon are jealous of Callirhoe's beauty, which all Persians admit is similar to Aphrodite's. At the trial at Artaxerxes's court Dionysius accuses Mithridates of trying to steal his wife and of forging a letter from Chaereas. After lengthy arguments Mithridates is acquitted of all wrongdoing, when he produces Chaereas in the flesh as the letter writer. Mithridates is released, but Artaxerxes is now in love with Callirhoe and makes her a ward of his wife, Statira.

Book 6. *The King and Callirhoe* + *Revolting Egyptians*.

Dionysius and Chaereas await the king's judgment to see which one will get Callirhoe, while the king schemes to acquire her for himself. The king's chief eunuch, Artaxates, tries by every means to force Callirhoe to renounce both her husbands and enter the king's harem. Just when the pressure is mounting on Callirhoe, the king is totally distracted by an announcement of a revolt of the Egyptians against his government. As the king marches off to war to meet the Egyptians, he instructs Statira to accompany him and to bring Callirhoe along. End of Act III.

Book 7. *Every Lover is a Warrior.*

Chaereas is so determined to strike out at Artaxerxes, he joins the forces of the revolting Egyptians, is given command of a group of Greek mercenaries, and captures the impregnable fortress of Tyre. The king meanwhile has left Statira and Callirhoe on the island of Aradus to protect them, and he has awarded Callirhoe to Dionysius for bravery on the battlefield. Chaereas is so successful with the army that he is given command of the navy and almost immediately captures Aradus, but he is unaware that Callirhoe is there. The Egyptian army, now lacking Chaereas, folds and surrenders to the Persian forces.

Book 8. *All's Well That Ends Well.*

It is not long before Chaereas discovers Callirhoe. Before Chaereas resigns his command, he offers a home in Syracuse to all his sailors who wish it, and then graciously returns Statira to Artaxerxes. For her part Callirhoe has developed feelings of guilt toward Dionysius and their son. She gives over her son to him to raise but fails even at the end to tell him the boy is Chaereas's. The reunited couple returns triumphantly to Syracuse, Chaereas retells the whole story to the citizenry assembled in the theatre, and Callirhoe visits the temple of Aphrodite to give thanks.

II *Extant Examples of Greek Novels*

Because of the recent revival of interest in ancient Greek novels, and also because of their relative inaccessibility, and, in addition, because the reader will want and need to view *The Adventures of Chaereas and Callirhoe* in the perspective of the few remaining extant examples of Greek novels, we will provide here a short series of summaries of these.

A. *Xenophon of Ephesus*
An Ephesian Tale: The Adventures of Anthia and Habrocomes

Book 1. In Ephesus on the coast of Asia Minor live two beautiful young people, Anthia and Habrocomes. The beauty of the young man Habrocomes is so great that he despises Eros, a tragic flaw, for the god shows Anthia to him and he falls deeply in love. The two lovers fall ill from unfulfilled love, but an oracle of Apollo convinces their parents the youths should marry. Once married, the couple travel south from Ephesus to Rhodes and are captured by pirates, led by Corymbos, who takes them to Tyre and the pirate leader Apsyrtos. While Corymbos tries to win the affections of Habrocomes, another pirate, Euxinos, attempts to entice Anthia.

Book 2.   Our hero and heroine are resolved on a double suicide, but are rescued by Apsyrtos who wants to sell them for a profit. Manto, Apsyrtos's daughter, falls in love with Habrocomes, but when she is rejected, accuses him in front of her father of attempted rape. He is tortured and incarcerated; Manto is married off to Moeris, a Syrian, and Anthia is given to her as a slave in her new home in Syria. To add insult to injury Manto forces Anthia to cohabit with a goatherd—unknown to Manto is the fact that the goatherd honors the chastity of Anthia. Meanwhile, back in Tyre Apsyrtos learns of his daughter's deceit and frees Habrocomes, appointing him steward of his house. The plot thickens when Manto learns that Moeris has fallen in love with Anthia. Manto orders the goatherd to kill Anthia, but he has no stomach for it and sells her to some Cilician merchants, in whose company she is captured by a highwayman named Hippothoos. When Habrocomes learns of Anthia's sale, he sets out to find her in Cilicia. But in this ever thickening plot we discover that Perilaos, chief constable of the area, has attacked Hippothoos and seized Anthia, and that Hippothoos has become a traveling companion of Habrocomes.

Book 3.   Habrocomes and Hippothoos journey into Cappadocia before the former learns from the latter that Anthia is alive in Cilicia. Perilaos meanwhile has fallen in love with Anthia, who is unable to continue to put him off, but who persuades a physician named Eudoxos to give her a deadly poison and so extricate her from her present perils. The prescribed drug is not lethal, and after some hours Anthia awakes to find herself entombed by her would-be husband. Grave robbers promptly make their way into her tomb, snatch her, and sell her in Alexandria to Psammis. News of all this comes to Habrocomes who follows her to Egypt, but there he is sold as a slave to Araxos and his lecherous wife, Bitch, who is so taken by Habrocomes that she kills her husband and proposes to him. Bitch's offer is rejected by a stunned Habrocomes, who is quickly jailed for killing Araxos on evidence supplied by Bitch.

Book 4. Habrocomes is tried and crucified in Pelusium in northern Egypt but the cross falls down; he is placed on a pyre but the Nile River extinguishes the flames. His execution is stayed. Meanwhile, in another part of Egypt Hippothoos recaptures Anthia but does not recognize her. One of Hippothoos's men and good friend is killed by Anthia as she protects her chastity; for this crime she is thrown into a pit with killer dogs, who, however, do not harm her because another brigand (in love with Anthia) throws meat to them daily.

Book 5. The ruler of Egypt sends Polyidos against Hippothoos, who is as wily as ever and escapes. Polyidos seizes Anthia, however, and falls in love with her, only to arouse the jealousy of his wife Rhenaia, who has Anthia sold to a brothel keeper in Tarentum in southern Italy. Habrocomes, having been freed in Egypt when it was learned that he was no murderer, sails to Syracuse and has a rather strange adventure with a necrophiliac. As fate would have it, Hippothoos is also staying in Sicily in Taormina—all of the principals are now located in southern Italy. Because Anthia does not work well in the brothel, she is sold to Hippothoos, who happens to be in Tarentum and recognizes her. He is determined to return her to her home in Ephesus and on the long journey home stops at Rhodes, to which place Habrocomes had also come as he journeyed home. Through the good graces of the deity Isis, our hero finds our heroine, and they live happily ever after.

Xenophon's novel is very close in plot to that of Chariton. The next Greek novel *An Ethiopian Adventure* is much more involved and rhetorical than Chariton's work, and it is visible to all how far it has moved away from the first novel.

B. *Heliodorus*
An Ethiopian Adventure: The Adventures of Theagenes and Chariclea

Book 1. This story starts *in medias res* at the mouth of the Nile where a group of highwaymen watch two young lovers, Theagenes and Chariclea, recovering from some kind of struggle. The outlaw leader, Thyamis, appears and takes the lovers captive back to his camp. There Cnemon attends to their needs and tells the delightful story of his Potiphar's wifelike stepmother, who caused him so much trouble. Because of a dream Thyamis is now so in love with the beautiful Chariclea that he wants an immediate marriage, but is put off temporarily by Chariclea. Another group of robbers approaches and Chariclea is hidden for protection in a cave. Thyamis is so distracted by love and jealousy that he stabs Chariclea, and is in turn himself captured by the new band of thieves.

Book 2. It turns out that Thyamis did not stab Chariclea but Thisbe, the evil servant of Cnemon's stepmother; Chariclea appears unharmed. It is decided that Thermouthis, the lover of Thisbe, and Cnemon will search for Thyamis. Cnemon meets the seer Calasiris at Chemmis near the Nile and is told about the adventures of the latter, his trip to Delphi, and his meeting with the priest of Apollo, Charicles, who tells Calasiris a long story.

Book 3. Calasiris speaks at length about religious rituals at Delphi and how at one of these Theagenes and Chariclea meet and fall in love. After Calasiris experiences a prophetic dream, Theagenes comes to him and tells him of his love for Chariclea.

Book 4. For Cnemon's (and the reader's) benefit Calasiris continues to unfold his story of events at Delphi. Charicles, priest of Apollo at Delphi, presents Calasiris with the blanket in which the baby Chariclea was wrapped when she was found. The embroidery worked on the blanket is that of Persinna, queen of Ethiopia. Calasiris relates how it came about that he knew Persinna and his interest in Chariclea. Theagenes, Chariclea, and Calasiris escape from Delphi with Phoenician sailors to search for home.

Book 5. After listening to Calasiris's story, Cnemon finds Chariclea in his house at Chemmis and learns that she and Theagenes have been separated; she was saved by a merchant friend of Calasiris, Nausicles, who on payment of a ransom surrenders Chariclea. Calasiris now continues his story of the journey from Delphi to Ethiopia, the stopover at Zacynthus, and their capture by the pirate Trachinus at the mouth of the Nile. Trachinus and his first lieutenant, Pelorus, argue over who should marry Chariclea, and a terrible fight ensues. The end of the fight is described at the beginning of Book 1.

Book 6. Cnemon, who has had many sad experiences with women, marries Nausicles's daughter. Chariclea and Calasiris start out in search of Theagenes, who is at Memphis in the care of Oroondates, and stumble on a recent battle site heaped with corpses. They oversee the despicable acts of a ghoulish sorceress.

Book 7. Calasiris settles a dispute in Memphis between his sons, a dispute made worse by the licentious actions of Arsace, wife of the Egyptian satrap, Oroondates. In Memphis Chariclea finds Theagenes, but Arsace also has designs on him. She tries to seduce him with the help of Cybele, her servant. Cybele's son, Achaemenes, is eager to marry Chariclea. Theagenes confesses that Chariclea is not his sister (shades of Abraham and Sarah). Calasiris dies.

Book 8. War breaks out between Oroondates and Hydaspes, king of the Ethiopians, over certain emerald mines. Achaemenes meanwhile tries to win over Chariclea as Arsace does Theagenes. Oroondates is cognizant of Arsace's character. Cybele tries to poison Chariclea and so remove her mistress's main obstacle to Theagenes, but she mistakenly drinks the poison. Chariclea is imprisoned for the murder of Cybele. Oroondates summons Theagenes and Chariclea from Memphis, but they are captured by Ethiopian soldiers near Syene. Arsace hangs herself.

Book 9.   Hydaspes seizes the city of Syene, but Oroondates and his Persian forces escape, only to regroup and attack Syene. In a great battle Hydaspes is again victorious, and now spares the life of Oroondates, but Theagenes and Chariclea are appointed as human sacrifices to commemorate the military victory.

Book 10.   The victorious king of Ethiopia is given a triumphal welcome in his capital city of Meroë. It is the wish of all the people that a human sacrifice be made to solemnize the great victory over the Persians. After Theagenes and Chariclea pass their chastity tests, they are accepted as worthy sacrificial victims. Chariclea protests that she cannot be sacrificed because she is not a foreigner and also because she is the daughter of a king. Various signs are given against sacrificing Chariclea, and with the populace demanding her freedom, Hydaspes releases her. Theagenes shows that he is someone special when he catches a runaway bull and defeats an Ethiopian giant in hand-to-hand combat. Charicles, the priest of Apollo at Delphi, now appears and accuses Theagenes of stealing his ward, Chariclea. Confronted with all this evidence, Hydaspes is convinced of Chariclea's birth and name, and he consents to the marriage of Theagenes and Chariclea.

Heliodorus's work is much more complex and meandering than those of Chariton and Xenophon, but the reader can nevertheless recognize even in this brief outline their affinities. Longus's *Daphnis and Chloe* stands apart from the first three and should be understood to be a type of pastoral novel.

C.   *Longus*
Daphnis and Chloe

Book 1.   In a short introduction Longus explains that his novel is not entirely an imaginative work but is rather an *ecphrasis*, a rhetorical description of a painting found in Lesbos. A goatherd named Lamon and his wife Myrtale find an exposed baby boy being suckled by a goat, rescue him, and name him Daphnis. Two years later a shepherd named Dryas and his wife Nape find an exposed baby girl being suckled by an ewe, rescue her, and name her Chloe. So at fifteen Daphnis becomes a goatherd and at thirteen Chloe a shepherdess. By constant association they fall in love, but since neither is acquainted with the mechanics of lovemaking their love comes to no fruition. Dorcon, a local cowherd, who knows all about sex acts, falls in love with Chloe. Emotional strains, which cannot be released, arise between Daphnis and Chloe. By presents of all kinds Dorcon tries to bribe Chloe and, failing in this, attempts to use force. One day pirates come and steal Dorcon's sheep, kill Dorcon, and seize Daphnis. By playing Dorcon's pipe and recalling the cattle which had been forced aboard the pirates' ship, Chloe effects a panic and capsizing of the ship. Daphnis escapes. Later back in camp the two youngsters are stirred sexually by nude bathing, but neither understands his feelings or knows the secret of their release.

Book 2. Daphnis and Chloe had met first in spring, but now it is fall, the vintage is being collected, and the people are full of thoughts about harvest festivals. Philetas, a local cowherd, who is a special friend of Eros, tries to tell Daphnis and Chloe about himself and his own special love Amaryllis: "The only releases of love are kissing, hugging, and lying together naked." Still Daphnis and Chloe do not understand. Young men from Methymna carry fun and games too far and get in trouble with the local shepherds. They return home and stir up the populace against Mytilene, the city near these shepherds's fields. The people of Methymna send out a war party and capture many flocks and also take Chloe aboard. But Pan, the god of all shepherds, comes to the aid of Chloe and causes panic in the forces of Methymna until they release her. The shepherds celebrate the victory and the fall festival: Daphnis and Chloe pledge eternal love.

Book 3. Winter descends on the pastoral scene, but Daphnis does a lot of hunting near Chloe's cottage and so gets to see her. A local, old farmer, named Chromis, has married a young girl, Lycaenion, who is in no way satisfied sexually by him. She has designs on Daphnis and has already perceived that he is a sexual novice and is determined to instruct him. Though she

wastes no time in giving Daphnis firsthand instruction and opening his eyes, he remains afraid to use his newly found skills on
the tender Chloe. Suitors in droves are now asking for Chloe's
hand in marriage, but Dryas puts them all off, knowing that
Chloe is really some noblewoman. Besides, none of the local
shepherds can offer a large dowry. The nymphs provide Daphnis
with three thousand drachmas for a dowry and an autumn wedding is planned. Lamon tries to postpone the wedding because
he is sure that Daphnis is some nobleman's son who was exposed
and that he should be married to a noblewoman. But Lamon and
Dryas do not confide in each other.

Book 4. Dionysophanes, the owner of Lamon's estate, and his
wife Cleariste plan a visit to their properties, which are especially prepared for the inspection. Lampis, a neighbor of Lamon,
ruins his garden in hope that Dionysophanes would withhold his
approval of Daphnis's marriage to Chloe—since he himself loves
Chloe so much. Dionysophanes' son, Astylus, and his son's
constant hanger-on, Gnathon, arrive before the parents do.
Gnathon makes repeated homosexual attempts on Daphnis, which
are repulsed with vigor. The master is pleased with Lamon's
care of his estate and with Daphnis's work, and under constant
persuasion from Gnathon decides to take Daphnis back to
Mytilene with him. But Lamon has learned what sort of a man
Gnathon is, and he is moved to reveal to Dionysophanes the
circumstances of Daphnis's birth and the tokens found with
the exposed child. Dionysophanes and his wife recognize the
tokens as those belonging to their baby which they had exposed.
They claim Daphnis as their son. Meanwhile, Lampis grabs
Chloe and takes her to his house, believing no one any longer
wants her. Gnathon, however, sees here a chance to redeem himself, and in a lightning attack recovers Chloe for Daphnis from
Lampis's house. Dryas now tells the story of how he found
Chloe as an exposed child. In Mytilene Dionysophanes finds
that a certain Megacles is Chloe's real father. Daphnis and Chloe
marry, and Daphnis finally gets a chance to practice some of
the things that Lycaenion had taught him some time before.
   The most striking difference between Longus's work and the
others is that there are no travel or journey elements and motifs.

Also, Daphnis is unfaithful to Chloe. In Chariton, Xenophon, and Heliodorus this would have been unthinkable.

D. *Achilles Tatius*
The Adventure of Leucippe and Cleitophon

Book 1. Achilles Tatius happens to be visiting in Sidon in Phoenicia and is particularly taken by a painting of Europa and the bull, when a young man named Cleitophon approaches and says that he knows all about the power of Eros. Cleitophon and his father, Hippias, live in Tyre, and the former is betrothed to his paternal half sister, Calligone. Cleitophon has an uncle, aunt, and cousin, named respectively Sostratus, Panthea, and Leucippe. Because of unsettled political conditions in Byzantium, Sostratus sends his wife and daughter to live with his brother Hippias in Tyre, where the daughter and Cleitophon fall in love. But Cleitophon is clumsy in matters of love and turns to his cousin Clinias for help, who is having a homosexual affair with a very pretty boy named Charicles. Clinias gives Cleitophon much advice on gentleness and manner; meanwhile, his own world collapses with the death of Charicles in a horse riding accident.

Book 2. Cleitophon begins to play all sorts of little games lovers play to attract the attention of the opposite sex. Cleitophon's servant Satyrus has become the lover of Leucippe's maid Clio, and the two slaves contrive to bring the lovers together frequently. Hippias is now very eager that Cleitophon should marry Calligone and makes all the preparations. Meanwhile, back in Byzantium a young man named Callisthenes has fallen in love with Leucippe, though he has never seen her. He is appointed special envoy to Tyre and while there steals Calligone, thinking she is Leucippe. Cleitophon now has a free hand with Leucippe, and Satyrus makes all the preparations for Cleitophon to spend the night with Leucippe. However, at the critical moment Panthea breaks in and Cleitophon escapes. Though Leucippe professes her continued virgin status, Panthea does not believe her. It seems best to the young people to leave Tyre at this time, and with Clinias in attendance Leucippe,

Cleitophon, Satyrus, and Clio escape to Sidon and there board a boat for Alexandria in Egypt. On this ship they make the acquaintance of one Menelaus, who is just escaping a very sad homosexual love affair. A lengthy discussion ensues, with Clinias and Menelaus defending homosexual love and Cleitophon heterosexual.

Book 3.   In a bad storm at sea the crew deserts the ship and the passengers come to shore at Pelusium. But Cleitophon and Leucippe are separated from Menelaus, Satyrus, and Clinias. On their way to Alexandria the young lovers are set upon by robbers, who take Leucippe to the robber chief to serve as a virgin sacrifice, but Cleitophon escapes and joins a regiment of soldiers who are about to attack these same robbers. As the two opposing groups line up for battle Cleitophon observes the robbers preparing Leucippe as a human sacrifice. They tie her up, cut out her entrails, and place them on an altar. The army regiment does not attack, however, because they are outnumbered two to one by the robbers. Later the next night Menelaus and Satyrus come to Cleitophon and bring along Leucippe! It seems that Menelaus and Satyrus had been Leucippe's murderers but had used stage swords which never hurt her.

Book 4.   As it happens the general of the regiment, one Charmides, has fallen in love with Leucippe and puts pressure on Menelaus to deliver the girl. Just as things begin to get sticky, Charmides is ordered to attack the robber band, and in the ensuing battle is killed. Leucippe next acquires a most peculiar lover named Gorgias, a kind of mad druggist who mistakenly gives her an undiluted aphrodisiac, driving her mad. A friendly man named Chaereas approaches and offers an antidote which restores Leucippe. While a new army arrives and destroys the robbers, the reader is given a description of two rare Egyptian animals, the hippopotamus and the crocodile.

Book 5.   Cleitophon and Leucippe move on to Alexandria where Chaereas plans to steal Leucippe. He hires a pirate band which seizes her and makes its escape by boat. Cleitophon pursues, but as he approaches the pirates decapitate Leucippe and throw her body into the sea. Cleitophon wastes the next six months mourning in Alexandria, but does recover his old friend and cousin Clinias, who informs him that only a few days after he and Leucippe had fled from Tyre, Sostratus, Leucippe's father, had given his consent to his marrying her. Cleitophon curses cruel fortune. In Alexandria a woman named Melite, who had lost her husband at sea, has fallen in love with Cleitophon and begs him to marry her. He consents to the marriage, but not until they arrive back in Ephesus, Melite's home. Melite pleads with him day and night to make her his wife. Back in Ephesus Melite befriends a mistreated slave who was sold to Melite's steward Sosthenes by certain pirates. The young slave turns out to be Leucippe who accuses Cleitophon of unfaithfulness with Melite, but is later convinced of his virginity. Melite's husband, Thersander, who had been thought dead, races into his house and proceeds to beat Cleitophon. Thersander moves out of the house, and Melite learns that her newest slave is in reality Leucippe. Nevertheless, Melite holds Cleitophon to his promise to make love to her when they reached Ephesus; Cleitophon obliges.

Book 6. Melite helps Cleitophon escape from her house, but he runs almost immediately into Thersander and his friends who have Cleitophon thrown into jail for adultery and theft. Sosthenes is the instigator of all this because he hates Melite, who had taken Leucippe from him. Next Sosthenes tells Thersander about Leucippe, and soon Thersander is eager to have her for his own. Sosthenes promptly arranges for Leucippe to be kidnapped and held in a small cottage to await Thersander's coming. At the beginning Thersander is gentle, but since Leucippe is insistent upon her virginity remaining intact, he becomes violent. At the same time he is angry with Melite for her adultery with Cleitophon. Melite, however, claims she has always been faithful and that Sosthenes has fabricated the whole story to malign her.

Book 7. Thersander plots to remove Cleitophon from the scene, and to achieve his end places a spy in his cell. After a time this spy "happens" to mention that he knows that Melite has had

Leucippe killed. If Cleitophon believes it, he will despair of ever seeing Leucippe and despise Melite—thus allowing Thersander to have both women. Cleitophon believes it. Once in the courtroom Cleitophon confesses that he and Melite killed Leucippe. This confession dooms him to death (which he can share with Leucippe) and also avenges Leucippe's murder on Melite. Clinias tells the true story but is not believed; Sosthenes who knows the true story runs away, and Cleitophon is condemned to death. But Sostratus, Leucippe's father, appears in Ephesus and forces the officials to stop torturing Cleitophon. At the same time Leucippe, who is no longer guarded by Sosthenes, escapes and races to Ephesus where she meets Cleitophon and her father.

Book 8.   By making the most noise and crying for Cleitophon's execution, Thersander hopes to deflect attention from himself. The two come to blows. At dinner Sostratus and Cleitophon exchange stories and bring everyone up to date. The next day we return to the courtroom where Thersander continues his tirade against Cleitophon and Melite. The defense attorney discloses many evil actions in Thersander's past. Finally, Leucippe is given a virginity test which she of course passes, proving herself a worthy bride and not a slave in Thersander's household. A virginity test is also administered to Melite, who of course cannot pass it, but who adds one stipulation to the rules: that she was faithful while Thersander was gone. She passes the test because she was unfaithful while Thersander was at home. Thersander is sent into exile, and Cleitophon and Leucippe live happly ever after.

Even to the casual reader it is obvious that each of the above novels is unique but nevertheless has many affinities to the other works. Chariton has built the most direct plot with the least surprises and least number of episodes. He relies much more on character development and causal actions and reactions. Rare is the happening or event which takes place without first establishing proper background material. Heliodorus and Achilles Tatius stress episodes, surprise events, puzzles, and shocking descriptions. Longus's first concern is with the scenery, on which he relies to set the stage and particularize the atmosphere. With regard to language, Chariton's is the most simple, unadorned, and unaffected. To go along with his simple style, Chariton employs the fewest digressions, which Heliodorus and Achilles Tatius use to flesh out their weaker plots and give some relief to unbroken strings of episode upon episode.

CHAPTER 4

Analysis of
The Adventures of Chaereas and Callirhoe

I *Introduction: Historical Perspectives*

HAD Chariton been trying to write a kind of history or historical reflections of the fifth-fourth-century B.C. Greek world, we could fault him for tampering with facts, confusing rulers, and failure to understand the great movements of peoples and events. On the other hand, however, in antiquity even the great Greek historian Herodotus and the eminent Roman historian Livy were most interested in conveying an overall impression or reflection of the period under consideration. Such criticism would hardly be appropriate here, for Chariton places his work within the genre of prose fiction and then gives it an appropriate dramatic and historical setting in time and place; he goes on to name names. It is obvious that he is not writing of his own age, the age of iron Romans, but of the Golden Age of Greece. In our survey of the historical aspect of Chariton's dramatic world, we are not seeking to push back the boundaries of darkness or even to find the earliest date or the latest possible date for Chariton himself. That task awaits other men.

Just as soon as Chariton has introduced himself and his subject in the first chapter of Book 1, we learn something about Hermocrates, father of the heroine: he is the very one who as head of the Syracusan forces defeated the Athenian expeditionary forces in 413 B.C. near Syracuse, in what must rank as one of the most tragic (in the wider sense) of all battles between countrymen. Hermocrates' rival for power at Syracuse was Ariston, father of the novel's hero, Chaereas. According to Thucydides (6.35-41), the chief domestic opponent of Hermocrates was one Athenagoras. But this apparent contradiction is not damaging to Chariton's story. The person of Hermocrates sets the dramatic date and milieu; the exact name of his rival (perhaps he had many others), who after all did not defeat the Athenians, adds nothing to the story. For Chariton's novel it is most important, however, to provide both heroine and hero with famous and noble, if unhistorical, parents. Chariton might, on the other hand, be confusing Ariston the Syracusan (unhistorical) with Ariston of Corinth, of whom Thucydides (7.39) has high praise as a naval captain in the Syracusan battle against Athens.

The next name of historical importance to meet us in the novel is Dionysius (Bk. 2), governor of Miletus, a port city in southwestern Asia Minor, to which Callirhoe had been taken by force. Chariton describes Miletus as a city owing allegiance to the Persian king. It is not clear whether Chariton describes Miletus after its revolt in 412 B.C. or as a partially free city within the Persian empire. His description of Miletus is somewhat confusing.

Dionysius falls in love with our heroine Callirhoe and believes that she is pregnant with his child; in fact it is Chaereas's. Before Callirhoe leaves Asia Minor and returns to Syracuse with Chaereas, she entrusts the raising of her child to Dionysius of Miletus. This is an extraordinary episode and peculiar in view of Callirhoe's strong instincts of love for her child. Perhaps Chariton is here following a tradition or myth about Callirhoe which requires him to write this episode. Or we could have at this point an historical intrusion or contamination. Chariton knew of another Dionysius, an historical one, Dionysius I, who was ruler of Syracuse (405-367 B.C.), had married an unnamed daughter of Hermocrates, and then succeeded Hermocrates to the highest position of power. The infant son of Callirhoe and Dionysius of Miletus surely took his father's name, Dionysius. Chariton tells us (2.9-11) that this son of Callirhoe will one day return to Syracuse, meet Hermocrates, and (it is implied by Chariton) succeed him as Dionysius I, tyrant of Syracuse. According to Chariton then, Callirhoe's son and not her husband will follow after Hermocrates. The many occurrences in Greek history of the name Dionysius make this historical section of Chariton's work very difficult to construe. Then too, our writer may have been following a written source of the legends of Hermocrates' family, or perhaps even a legend of Callirhoe.

Another historical contamination may lie hidden under that peculiar episode (Bk. 1, Chap. 4) in which Chaereas kicked Callirhoe in the stomach (she was pregnant and did not lose the child, indicating that the severity of the kick was slight and that she fainted from the horror of it, not its force). The action of kicking his wife is too much out of character for Chaereas who does nothing like that, or any other rash act even resembling that, in the whole book. Like Callirhoe's giving her child to Dionysius, Chaereas's kicking is obviously a literary contamination brought in from some unknown source which Chariton followed. Chariton failed, however, to integrate these deeds of his leading actors into the makeup of their character or rationalize them as being consistent with his actors' other deeds. Braun suggests that Chariton added the episode of kicking for one of two possible reasons. First, Chariton imitated Herodotus in many places, and this is one of the stories told in Herodotus (3.32) and borrowed by Chariton. Second, Chariton used the story told by Herodotus but trusted that his readers would see behind it the recent death of Nero's pregnant wife, Poppaea, who was kicked to death by the emperor.

Evidence to support or deny the existence at this time of a satrap of Caria named Mithridates (Bk. 3) is very thin. But the historian Ctesias, to whom veracity is no more a paramount virtue than it is to Chariton, records that Statira, wife of Artaxerxes Mnemon, made one Mithridates a satrap. Chariton introduces us also to two famous historical personages in Babylon, King Artaxerxes Mnemon (Artaxerxes II) and his beautiful wife Statira (Bks. 4 and 5). When Chaereas and Callirhoe sailed from Syracuse, they left Hermocrates alive; we know he died in 408 B.C. When Callirhoe arrived in Babylon she found Artaxerxes Mnemon on the throne. We know that he ruled from 404-363 B.C. (or 358 B.C.). Some years later when Chaereas and Callirhoe returned to Syracuse, they found Hermocrates still alive. By all historical reckoning he should have been dead. The twentieth-century mind in its quest for truth is satisfied only when it knows the names and dates of all the players. Chariton, on the other hand, delighted to focus his reader's attention at once on the character; we, on the other hand, do not care to study the character until we have him adequately classified. In attempting to put Chariton in the best light, we can see that the discrepancy in his chronological sequence is in error by no more than one generation.

The last historical event we wish to consider is the revolt of Egypt (Bks. 6, 7, 8) from Artaxerxes Mnemon's Persian empire; this revolt is the cause which effects the final reunion of Chaereas and Callirhoe. The French scholar Grimal claims that Chariton is so confused at this point that he has the Egyptians revolting under Artaxerxes II when they should have revolted under Artaxerxes I, who crushed their uprising in 455 B.C. The German scholar Schmid also thinks that Chariton is confused, but that he must mean the Egyptian revolt of 389-387 B.C. It would now be very difficult to ascertain to which Egyptian rebellion Chariton referred, because the Egyptians seem to have been in a constant state of rebellion from Persian rule. Artaxerxes Mnemon assumed the throne of Persia on the death of Darius in 404 B.C. Almost immediately his own brother Cyrus led a revolt against him, and, as Manetho tells us, Amyrtaeus II also rebelled and set up a separate kindom in Egypt which lasted six years. In all likelihood this is the revolt which plays such a large part in the work under consideration. Grimal and Schmid were apparently nodding. Chaereas joined in the revolt on the side of the Egyptians and took command of a band of three hundred Greek mercenaries who had already been in the fight. Chariton's report of Greek mercenaries fighting in the East agrees well with what other historians recorded. In his *Anabasis* Xenophon of Athens tells the story of ten thousand Greeks fighting for Cyrus against Artaxerxes Mnemon, and Cornelius Nepos tells us that the Athenian Chabrias (d. 357 B.C.) fought as a soldier of fortune for the Egyptian king.

While Chariton's use of historical materials is at times faulty in detail and annoying in its lack of specific references to time, place, people, or events, we must ask ourselves if he intended his work to be any different from what we have. Our conclusions must be that he wanted to give his novel a general historical setting with just enough specific detail and fact to put the action and characters in the familiar world, and to give an air of reality, but not so much that it could destroy the make-believe world into which the author slowly entices his readers.

Of the writers of imaginative prose fiction few had the unassuming honesty of Chariton to step forward and tell their stories without disguising them as something else. Lucian the satirist (b. 120 A.D.) took these writers to task in his *True History*. He singled out Ctesias (tragic historian), Iambulus, and Antonius Diogenes (romancers of a sort) for special scorn. They all write fiction, claims Lucian, but are hesitant to publish it in that form. They choose history or travelogues as a cover-up for fiction, and then are bold enough to claim the fictions are true because they themselves saw the events portrayed.

In an earlier section we spoke of this low repute in which prose fiction was held. It is difficult to appreciate all of Lucian's barbs hurled at the above three writers because their works are not extant. But we can look at the disguises of several novels that are extant (Cf: Chap. 3). In his novel *The Adventures of Leucippe and Cleitophon*, Achilles Tatius did not write the story on his own authority but claimed that he saw a painted picture of the whole tale, which one of the protagonists, Cleitophon, explained to him. This literary device, as mentioned above, is called *ecphrasis* and means literally a rhetorical explanation and exposition of a work of art. The author can cite good rhetorical precedent and escape the stigma that prose fiction carried. The history of *ecphrasis* goes back to Vergil and thence all the way to Homer. In his pastoral novel *Daphnis and Chloe*, Longus adopted a similar disguise as Achilles Tatius, and claimed that his prose work was really a verbalization of a splendid and moving painting he had seen in Lesbos.

The disarming simplicity and straightforward approach of Chariton to his subject and to his audience would have been welcomed by Lucian. It is hoped that the modern reader will feel the same.

II *The Drama in Five Acts*

Chariton probably intended for us to see *The Adventures of Chaereas and Callirhoe* as a work of prose fiction for the stage; hence, we will deal with it in those terms. It seems obvious that he presented his work to us as a series of dramatic or theatrical confrontations connected by enough narrative to tell a continuous story. Within each act he built up special dramatic scenes, which are not climaxes or false climaxes, but structures of particular tension which would work well as episodes on the stage. He tried to put together scenes where emotions were apparent; his descriptions were graphic and full of visual impact, which the reader was expected to translate to the theatre. In the theatre of today the spectators see all; nothing is left to their imagination. In the ancient Greek theatre almost no action took place on the stage which was reserved for verbal artistry. Action of any kind was reported to the audience by the chorus or one of the ubiquitous messengers. Recognizing this, Chariton knew that he could "stage" his novel because the audience (or reader) was accustomed to (or rather expected) to use its imagination for action scenes and then hear enough narrative to connect them.

The reader of Chariton's work should also be aware of his consistent attempts to stir the emotions of the reader. The contemporary American or European reader with his senses jaded by overexposure to violence, passion, and animal sex, will find here a weak appeal to his emotions. It is difficult to brush away centuries of the novel and look objectively at the first one. One of the emotions Chariton did try to awaken was curiosity and wonder (*admiratio*). Such is not in vogue in modern novels. He attempted to do this by presenting to the reader a series of *mirabilia*, descriptions of events and people worthy of stirring *admiratio* in the reader.

III   *Act I (Books 1-3.2): A Marriage Made in Heaven*

In a manner resembling Greek Old and New Comedy and also Roman Comedy, the narrator (frequently a slave in comedy, but here the author) stepped forward and introduced himself, his chief characters, and the nature of the work, as though it were a dramatic prologue:

My name is Chariton of Aphrodisias, secretary to Athenagoras the lawyer, and my story is all about a love affair that started in Syracuse. . . . There is this magnificent creature called Callirhoe . . . her beauty is known far and wide from where come her suitors—lords and princes. . . . And also there is this incredibly handsome young man, Chaereas, a veritable image of Achilles.

As soon as Chariton had taken his own bow, he moved immediately to the story, not like so many other ancient writers *in medias res*. Unlike Greek audiences who knew all the plots of tragedy and comedy, Chariton's audience had to be informed in detail right from the beginning. Chariton even had to explain who Hermocrates, Callirhoe's father and a famous general, was. This was not an enlightened fifth-century B.C. Athenian audience; it was a mixed group, culturally, socially, and economically. The detailed introduction was thus called for and in fact required.

Chariton pointed out that the fathers of the handsome leading actors were political rivals, and hinted that should their children become lovers, family feuds would stand in their way. We think immediately of Shakespeare's Capulets and Montagues and the tragedy of their children in *Romeo and Juliet*. As children of politically important people in Syracuse, Chaereas and Callirhoe naturally took part in the festival of Aphrodite which included a public procession (Bk. 1, Chap. 1). We must remember that Greek women did not usually appear in public except at religious functions or public sacrifices. Marriages were arranged by family contracts, but the progress of the story and the love-at-first-sight episode required a physical encounter. Chariton was either not interested in pursuing the family feud or lacked the technical skill to handle one story with two main plots. We are the poorer for it.

The shy Callirhoe and the athletic Chaereas meet as the procession of boys walks by that of young girls; it was love at first sight, if what they experienced can be called love. Perhaps admiration is a choicer word. Love at first sight is a motif we will see repeated by Anthia and Habrocomes in Xenophon of Ephesus and by Achilles in Dictys's *Romance of Troy* (Bk. 3.2); the motif of lovers meeting first in religious settings is found also in Xenophon of Ephesus and in Callimachus's *Acontius and Cydippe* (see also Parthenius 1.1 and 32.2). It seems that Chariton was operating within a literary tradition. In each

other Chaereas and Callirhoe recognized immediately nobility
and virtue. These qualities were apparent from their faces and
radiated from their eyes. Ancients believed, for better or worse,
in a study of appearances called physionomics, which was
raised to the level of a science: by the outward appearance of
an individual his fellowmen could judge his inner character,
virtues, and lineage. Aristocrats looked like aristocrats and were
separated by nature from lesser beings.[1]

Easily, perhaps too easily, Chariton wrote that the would-be
lovers met at a festival and procession for Aphrodite. It is
legitimate to ask, why at an Aphrodite festival? She was not a
patron deity of Syracuse; she was not a celebrated goddess in
the city; there were no major temples of Aphrodite in Syracuse.
A review of the topographical evidence shows no minor temple
of Aphrodite in Syracuse. Only deities considered important
in that city would have festivals of great splendor, which inci-
dentally had to be paid for by the public treasury. Because
the Greeks had so many deities in their pantheon, we tend
to overlook their individualistic natures and functions. But
Aphrodite *was* a major deity, worthy of a procession, and relevant to a story written by a man from Aphrodisias, where she was
the eponymous deity of the city. We thus would like to suggest
at the outset that, while Chariton set his story in Syracuse and
used famous people from it, he was actually thinking of Aphrodisias and transferred his personal experiences from there to
Syracuse. While this supposition is hard to support with hard
evidence, it does not seem that Chariton had any firsthand
knowledge of Syracuse, and in fact was mistaken to believe it
had a temple to Aphrodite. A glance at an ancient map of
Aphrodisias[2] shows that Chaereas, leaving either the amphi-
theatre or the baths, would naturally encounter on the narrow
residential streets a procession of girls leaving the temple of
Aphrodite. Such an encounter is hard to imagine in Syracuse.

The lovers met momentarily, exchanged glances, and immediately became love-sick. Chaereas was so taken by Callirhoe
that he was barely able to walk home, "wounded mortally as
though in battle." Callirhoe was so ashamed (like all true
maidens) and yet so in love she fell ill, not unlike Callimachus's
Cydippe. Chariton tells us the gods have arranged all this—the

chance meeting, falling in love, and the pain of love. It appears that Chaereas and Callirhoe were too beautiful and incurred the wrath, or at least hostility, of the gods. The technical term for such hostility is *phthonos*, a type of envy. Many in the ancient world (Herodotus and Sophocles being among the most famous) felt that a man who did not know himself (i.e., that he was *not* a god) was in danger of incurring the anger of the gods. King Midas would be a good example. Even after the lovers get together they move incessantly from one trouble to another, apparently the playthings of Fortune, but in reality the objects of the gods's *phthonos*.

The present situation with both lovers sick and separated because of family feuds is highly unstable. At this point of crisis the assembly of the people of Syracuse (in the role of the chorus of tragedy) by gentle persuasion convinced the lovers' fathers to allow that there be a wedding. Arrangements for the marriage were made, and since the bride had few rights, she was the last to learn of it:

"Her knees were unstrung and her heart stopped." On the spot she became speechless and a darkness poured over her eyes and she almost passed out . . . she recovered quickly . . . kissed Chaereas . . . and when she appeared in public, the assembled people were astonished and thought she was Artemis, the hunter goddess.

The opening line of the above quote Chariton took from *Iliad* 21; already in the first chapter of the first book Chariton associated his characters and novel with the epic tradition. This was continued in the second sentence above which was treated as a *formula* (i.e., a repeated phrase) in the best epic style. Each time the heroine was about to faint, Chariton employed this same phrase. In the last sentence Callirhoe was compared to Artemis; in the previous quoted section we saw that Chaereas was compared to Achilles. Chariton frequently compared his leading characters to mythical figures, and even certain situations, in which his characters found themselves, to situations from mythology. Because it is easily apparent that Chariton and the other Greek novelists relied very heavily on the use of elements from myth and epic for comparisons, descriptions, and metaphors, we will point out only what seems to be the best usages. Most of the analogues from myth in Chariton are illustrative, some symbolic, employed to try to heighten the reader's perception of the scene. "At their best they provide the vivid parallel—the graphic analogue—that enable the reader to visualize almost as if physically present either the person or the situation with which the author is concerned."[3]

The story goes on:

The wedding of Chaereas and Callirhoe was very similar to that of Peleus and Thetis which happened long ago in Pelion. The god of Envy was here as earlier the goddess Strife had been in Pelion.

The analogue from myth played an important and influential role here also. By comparing Thetis's wedding to Callirhoe's, Chariton not only represented the wedding of the latter as having the splendor of the former, but he also illustrated symbolically that Callirhoe's wedding was, like Thetis's, merely the starting point for a series of misfortunes for herself and her child. The analogue forebodes danger and bad luck. Chariton placed the god of Envy at the wedding of Callirhoe so that the reader should understand that the evil about to befall Callirhoe was due to the jealousy of certain gods because of her beauty. No further description of the wedding is given, nor does Chariton offer a picture of the wedding chamber and its blushing bride. Instead, the scene changes immediately, and we are given a picture of a group of suitors licking their wounds after losing Callirhoe. They were furious that she rejected them, and married Chaereas as soon as she had met him. One suitor in particular, the prince of Rhegium, was furious:

"If she had married one of us [suitors], I would not be so enraged. Suitors for the hand of a pretty girl win and lose, just like victors and losers in athletic games. Chaereas has affronted me by winning the race and not even entering the contest. We here pined away at her door and spent sleepless nights waiting to get a glimpse of her coming in or out; we bribed her attendants and nurses; we gave ourselves to her as slaves."

The motif of suitors waiting outside the door of a young girl's house was well-used by classical writers from the fourth century B.C. to the first century A.D. A lover who pined away at his mistress's door was called an *exclusus amator,* or locked-out lover. It is such a popular motif and one with such a long history that Frank Copley was able to devote an entire book to tracing it through classical literature.[4] Copley has isolated seven variable ingredients which constitute the maximum number of elements in the *exclusus amator* motif. Rarely will a writer use more than several of these in any one occurrence of the motif: (1) lover's passage through the streets; (2) repulse at the door; (3) lament of the lover; (4) drunkenness; (5) garland left at the door; (6) verses written at the doorway; and (7) lover's vigil at the locked door.

From the passage of Chariton quoted above, we can easily identify his use of the *exclusus amator* motif. This motif was reserved almost exclusively for poetry and drama-in-poetry; its employment here in prose points to Chariton's desire to associate his work with the poetic mode. The motif of the lover's constant attention and commitment of himself as his mistress's slave will bear fruit many centuries later in the romances of courtly love; the idea that a group of suitors are contestants like athletes in a game will bear fruit in those same centuries as jousts.

As a group, the former suitors of Callirhoe were hurt, offended, and even ashamed, and they plotted to take vengeance on the newly married pair. Because of the power of Hermocrates in Syracuse, they planned to attack under disguise, and then, not against Callirhoe who was "not the kind to think low thoughts," but against Chaereas who "was trained in the gymnasia, has no experience in love, and [is] an easy target for jealousy." Chaereas, according to plan, was called out of town to his father's estate where it was reported that Ariston was hurt. Callirhoe was left at the new couple's house (as was fitting), and Chaereas ran to aid his father. While he was absent, the bitter suitors at night decorated Callirhoe's doorway with wreaths and garlands, sprinkled perfumes all around, poured much wine on the ground, and set around half-burned torches. All of these were traditional witnesses of a nightlong vigil of *exclusi amatores* and also of wild orgies. Chaereas returned shortly, and on seeing the scene, imagined the worst and accosted Callirhoe and accused her of unfaithfulness. For her part she literally shamed him into changing his first impressions. It is obvious, however, that this quick temper and jealousy on the part of Chaereas is a foreshadowing of evil to come. The suitors saw this quality in Chaereas even before Callirhoe recognized it. The suitors, led by the prince of Agrigentum, were not easily put off, however, and, operating under the same assumptions as expressed by Chariton that "a woman who thinks she is in love is easily duped by her boyfriend," first hired a young man to gain the confidence and bed of Callirhoe's most trusted maid, and then an old actor to work on the jealous nature of Chaereas. The young man arranged to come to Callirhoe's house late at night and gain admittance through the good offices of the captivated maid. At the same time the old actor got the ear of Chaereas and informed him, under the mask of reluctance, that his wife was unfaithful, that he was a cuckold, and that if he wanted proof all he had to do was to watch his front door late that night. Chaereas, the jealous, was completely taken in by the suitors' plan and set up the watch over his own door.

The motif of the jealous and suspicious husband, and sometimes of the cuckold, setting a trap for his wife was repeated often in late Latin and medieval literature. On seeing the young man enter his house, Chaereas could not endure the insult and rushed forward only to scare off the intruder before the scene took shape. Callirhoe was found sitting in the dark awaiting Chaereas, and she ran to meet him as he approached. He greeted her with a swift kick to the stomach which sent her sprawling:

Callirhoe lay on the floor and did not move. She exhibited all the signs of death. The whole population of Syracuse began to mourn, and the episode took on the appearance of the destruction of a famous city.

Chaereas tortured all the slaves until he sadly learned the truth; whereupon he attempted to kill himself but was prevented from so doing by Polycharmus, a friend, as Patroclus had been to Achilles.

The actors on the scene did not know that Callirhoe was alive, but the reader gets a hint that in fact she is. Chariton associated the present scene with a tragic episode from epic, the destruction of a city. Chaereas and Polycharmus became incarnate figures (analogues from myth) of Achilles and Patroclus. The vengeance contrived by the suitors against Chaereas is very similar to that of Don John, envious of Claudio's good fortune with Hero, in Shakespeare's *Much Ado About Nothing*. It is highly unlikely, however, that the Bard knew Chariton. On numerous occasions our hero Chaereas tried to kill himself; he made an attempt on his own life at least twice before Callirhoe was buried. The prominence and fascination with death or apparent instances of death cannot be laid entirely to Chariton's literary creativity and interests. The attractiveness of suicide was found at this time especially among the Stoics, who made almost a cult ritual out of it, and the Christians who sought out martyrdom by various open demonstrations.

A. D. Nock has studied this peculiar attitude of the upper, middle, and lower classes and attributes it to various popular attitudes: a general fascination with death; the widespread notion and belief that the body is a tomb (*sōma sēma*); pessimism and a feeling that blind Fate rules the universe and, in particular, men's lives; the obsession surrounding suicide in legend and life; and finally, a desire for theatrical prominence, a desire to be noticed. In this section of Chariton and in those to follow, we see a predisposition and propensity for theatrical poses, in which disaster or near disaster always embraced thoughts of death. Our hero and heroine were ever prepared to die, to suffer all types of torments. Each one is quick to jump to the conclusion that, when anything goes amiss, his partner was dead but still chaste:

The Greek novel bears witness to the fascination exercised by the thought of invincible chastity and beautiful young persons facing pain with readiness, features which we will find later in the hagiographic romance.[5]

The murder was discovered immediately and Chaereas was indicted for murder. But he offered no defense; rather he condemned himself and asked to be stoned and thrown unburied into the sea. Hermocrates with no trace of malice understood apparently what happened and blamed it all on the criminal acts of the suitors. With Hermocrates at his side Chaereas was acquitted unanimously. It is worthwhile to note at this point the self-discipline exercised by Chariton in not presenting a full-blown courtroom scene full of speeches and distraught defendants. Greeks loved the actions of a court case, and litigation in Greek literature was a high-frequency motif. (Chariton did yield to the temptation of displaying his expertise in courtroom rhetoric in Bk. 5). Immediately after the acquittal, the efforts of all concerned focused on a magnificent funeral procession and burial in the rich splendor of gold and silver in a seaside tomb belonging to Hermocrates's family. This scene concluded with a foreboding remark by the author (i.e., the author and the reader alone knew what was happening):

Her tomb became a storehouse of rich treasure. But the gifts intended as an honor for the dead girl became instead the source of her future troubles.

In his description of Callirhoe's funeral Chariton had bystanders remark how much she looked like the sleeping Ariadne, which was not, however, merely another example of Chariton's analogues from myth. According to ancient stories, Ariadne, daughter of King Minor and Pasiphaë, helped Theseus escape the labyrinth after he had killed the Minotaur. After fleeing to the island of Naxos, Theseus abandoned Ariadne (while she slept), and Dionysus rescued and married her. Chariton here (1.6) pictured Callirhoe as the sleeping Ariadne (sleeping bride). At 3.3 he repeated the mythic analogue of Ariadne: Callirhoe was the stolen Ariadne (stolen bride). Dionysus, according to Chariton's version, had stolen Ariadne at Naxos. At 8.1 he again repeated the Ariadne motif: Callirhoe was compared with the forgotten Ariadne (forgotten bride) whom Theseus deserted. It is obvious from the frequency of comparisons between Ariadne and Callirhoe that the reader was intended to see Callirhoe as a type of Ariadne, and that while Callirhoe was a somewhat unfamiliar character she was brought into focus, universalized, and delineated nicely by the simile.

The plot of the story continued (1.7) with the introduction of Theron, a local pirate and cutthroat and his band of men, who determined to give up petty thefts and risk everything on one night's work of tomb-robbing. Theron had seen the riches buried with Callirhoe, and, with the promise of this great wealth, ordered his men to rob the tomb late at night. Digging tools and a boat were quickly made ready. The motif of suspended animation in which Callirhoe lived has a later parallel in Archistrates' daughter in *Apollonius of Tyre* (Chap. 24). Finally, Callirhoe awakened; she immediately recognized the inside of the tomb and remembered Chaereas's all but fatal kick. While bemoaning her fate, she wondered if Chaereas buried her so quickly because he had found another girl. It is one of the rare displays of jealously by Callirhoe. Shortly, she heard the tomb-robbers dig in and wondered if death in this grave was worse than what the villains outside had in store for her. The first robber rushed in only to be terrified by what he called a ghost. This graphic image of a spooky cemetery is a good example of Chariton's subtle humor. But Theron was a man of steel (and so was the sword he carried), and the tomb did not scare him. He walked in armed with a sword and brought Callirhoe out.

Theron realized that this girl would bring a good price in the slave market and announced that he would spare her, but a comrade disputed the wisdom of such an act:

"We already lead a dangerous life. You probably can sell her at a very handsome price, but let us rather take only the rich treasure from the tomb. The gold and silver have no eyes and tongue and will not tell anyone how we got them. Let us kill her here and now."

Theron was too greedy to heed the advice and, rejecting common sense, loaded the girl together with all the gold on board the waiting ship. From what is known from other sources tomb-robbers were a problem in the entire ancient world. Ancient tombs are today frequently upset by robbers, sometimes even by archaeologists. Pirates like Theron were another matter. Because pirates appear here and in most other ancient novels, but apparently had no real role in the first-second centuries A.D. when Chariton lived, we can suggest that Chariton was here making use of one of the genre's standard motifs, or else he added the pirates to give the story a late fifth-century B.C. Greek flavor.[6]

Theron was very solicitous about the health of his captive, as the pirates began their sea journey in the direction of Athens. He was constantly aware of the retail value of a well-kept maiden. Callirhoe began to feel sorry for herself and, without expressing openly her fear or dislike of Athens, said that she would rather die than be sold as a slave in Athens. We must remember that it was her father, as head of Syracusan forces, who so savagely routed the Athenians in 413 B.C. As the pirates continued to sail, they presently came near to the harbor at Athens, where many of the men wished to disembark and sell Callirhoe. Theron objected:

"Do not tell me that you do not know about the inquisitiveness, curiosity, and meddling of the men of Athens. They stand around all the time gossiping, suing people in court, grilling strangers and traders about everything under the sun. Athenian courts give us more to fear than those in Syracuse. We should rather go to Ionia [i.e., Asia Minor] where people are rich and know how to enjoy their wealth. Besides, I know people there."

Almost straight east of Athens lies Miletus on the coast of Asia Minor, where the pirates put into port. Actually they dropped anchor about ten miles from Miletus so that Theron could slip into the city without notice. Theron dared not sell Callirhoe openly because the whole transaction would have aroused too much suspicion—she was so beautiful everyone would have recognized her as a member of some noble family. As it happened, Dionysius, governor of Miletus, was walking through the city, and the crowd of people around him attracted Theron's attention. Theron quickly learned who the important personage was and that he had recently lost his wife. What a golden opportunity, thought Theron. After conversing with Leonas, Dionysius's chief steward and guardian of his only daughter, who was in the retinue of the great man, Theron mentioned that he had a truly lovely lady of Sybaris for sale who would make a good nurse for the child—better for Leonas that Dionysius get a nurse for the child than a stepmother! Leonas decided that it would be worth his effort at least to look at the girl and arranged with Theron to meet him at Dionysius's country home. At her entry into the manor Leonas thought that Aphrodite had come down to earth and he agreed to pay her full price even though Theron had no registration papers for her. He feared that Theron would get another buyer. For his part Theron set sail for the high seas before his tricks could be discovered.

While Callirhoe sat all alone in her bedroom, she bemoaned her sad state and rehearsed (for the audience) all that had happened to her in the preceding days. This is the conclusion of Book 1. As the curtain falls, we see a weary and discouraged Callirhoe fall asleep. In her summary of events which took her from her bridal chamber to Dionysius's house, Callirhoe described her journey as a travel from one tomb to another: (1) her bridal chamber became a tomb when Chaereas kicked her; (2) she was buried in the family tomb; (3) the hold of Theron's ship was for her a tomb; and (4) because she was a slave and prisoner in Dionysius's house, it was as good as a tomb for her. This final scene in which Callirhoe falls asleep, again in a kind of tomb, is the type of graphic image which ties Chariton closely to drama. It is also good Charitonian irony to place Callirhoe back into a type of tomb (slavery) from which her hero, Chaereas, will one day rescue her. The audience knows about this future rescue, but Callirhoe does not. From this arises the irony. The presentation of the entire first book stands surprisingly simple and straightforward, while just beneath the surface lies a persistent use of irony.

IV Act I (Book 2): The Courtship of Callirhoe

Having ordered his chief assistants, Phocas and wife Plangon, to care for Callirhoe, Leonas set out for Miletus to announce his purchase to Dionysius, who was in the proper erotic mood, having just seen a vision of his wife. Dionysius had felt a terrible sense of loss at the death of his wife, and the fact that he dreamed of her frequently reflected more on his character than it did on the chance coincidence of the announcement of Callirhoe's purchase together with the dream of his wife. Somewhat later in this book (2.9) Callirhoe will have a similar dream of Chaereas, and, while it did not have any erotic impetus as such, it did influence in a real sense Callirhoe's relationship to Dionysius. Chariton structured this book on two instances of the same efficient motif: the husband's dream of his dead wife inclined him toward a new marriage; the wife's dream of her lost husband convinced her to seek a new alliance. Dionysius listened to Leonas's story of Callirhoe's purchase but objected to certain inconsistencies in his story. His training and nobility opposed any connection he might have with a slave:

"Leonas, slavery and a truly beautiful person are mutually exclusive terms. Poets teach us the beautiful people are children of the gods and also of noblemen. You must certainly mean that she is beautiful when compared with local farmers' daughters. But I approve of the purchase."

When it was learned that Theron had already fled Miletus, Leonas was embarrassed by not being able to complete the transaction and have Callirhoe's purchase registered. Leonas's plans suffered at this point a small setback. Again we can see, through Dionysius's treatment of the Callirhoe affair, the strong relationship the ancient Greeks felt existed between the outer features of a person and his inner character and lineage. When the eye, the mirror of the soul, is beautiful, so is the soul. Beautiful inner character and outward features follow after a noble parentage only.

Meanwhile, back at Dionysius's country estate, Plangon, the wife of Phocas (chief assistant of Leonas) was seeing to the physical needs of Callirhoe. Standing in all her nude beauty, Callirhoe amazed even the maids of Dionysius's former wife:

"We thought Dionysius's first wife was a striking beauty. But she would hardly be worthy of acting as the servant of this girl."

The irony of this statement is apparent immediately. Without telling the reader in so many words, Chariton was allowing the maids to rate and compare their former mistress with the new one. From the disparity of understanding arises the irony. The subsequent troubles of Callirhoe, like her earlier ones, began with her excessive beauty; every man desired her and set in motion great forces, which she could not control, to get possession of her. Even the various deities of Love and their opposite Envy, harbor jealousy of Callirhoe (*phthonos*), as she says: "The goddess Aphrodite is the cause of all my troubles."

Plangon and Callirhoe visited the temple of Aphrodite, and

the latter prayed that her beauty, the source of great trouble, might never again please any man. Such a prayer, however, was a request opposed to the nature of that deity to whom she was praying and was rejected out of hand. Because she had seen a vision of Aphrodite the night before, Callirhoe returned to Aphrodite's temple, just ahead of Dionysius, a constant attendant at her temple. Dionysius had left Miletus and was preparing to visit his country estate, which bordered on Aphrodite's temple. Aphrodite's nature as a primeval force rather than as a sophisticated and enlightened deity was exposed here in her adamant refusal to honor the wishes of Callirhoe. As Dionysius entered the temple and saw Callirhoe for the first time, he was literally struck; he fell in love at first sight. Before Callirhoe could convince him differently, he assumed she was an epiphany of Aphrodite, and he dropped to the ground to worship her. It is unclear at this point if we are to understand that Callirhoe was as beautiful as Aphrodite, or that Aphrodite had "blinded" Dionysius with her own beauty. Perhaps both are intended. The latter case, however, would present Aphrodite as a maddening, unthinking force, determined to make all men bow to her beauty and will. (Aphrodite affected Paris in the same way and caused the Trojan War.) Dionysius left the temple and departed for his estate, but the damage had been done: he was wounded by madness and desire caused by Aphrodite. In this episode of love, as in many other similar situations, Chariton consistently employed religious terminology to describe erotic events. It was an artistic way of reinforcing the religious and erotic blend in the nature of Aphrodite.

Like the great man he was, Dionysius showed all the signs of royal breeding and discipline the ancients expected from princes. He went about his normal duties and dealt with his new slave Callirhoe as though she were any other of his possessions. But his emotions almost tore apart that fine outer facade:

Though it was late at night Dionysius could get no sleep. His mind remained fixed in the temple of Aphrodite, as he recalled every detail of the person of Callirhoe. Even her tears aroused him. The battle between reason and passion was visible in his eyes; though his thoughts remained fixed on the matter of Callirhoe, his actions befitted a nobleman. He reasoned thus with himself: "Dionysius, prince of Ionia . . . are you not ashamed to act like a schoolboy in the midst of his first love affair . . . while you are in fact still mourning your dead wife? Are you not ashamed to come to your country estate, to wear your funeral dress in public, all as a disguise to allow you to marry without notice a second wife, who is a slave and whose chattel title you do not hold?"

Eros attacked Dionysius relentlessly until he was forced to go to Leonas to learn every bit of information known about Callirhoe. Leonas pretended not to know how deep the prince's feelings for his new slave went, and offered all his information about the case, and also offered to bring her to his rooms. At this point we get our first real glimpse at the high moral character and discipline of Dionysius. His restraint and refusal to order her at their first meeting in the temple into his bed gave a hint of his ethical bearing. On the next morning he arranged to meet her in the temple of Aphrodite but took along slaves as witnesses. He was again struck by her beauty; but after a long, clumsy, and uneasy silence, he begged her to tell the story of how she came to Miletus. Reluctantly, she gave her name but refused any more detailed information, claiming it in no way could be believed because of her present lowly state in life. Hinting that it would not alter his opinion of her even if he learned she had committed a heinous crime, the prince made his first mistake. She struck out at him immediately, eliciting a type of apology, and then continued to tell the whole story from her spurious death to her sale as slave in Miletus. An interesting omission is any mention of Chaereas: there is the intriguing possibility that it is a "Freudian omission," signaling an unconscious desire for the prince; or perhaps the exclusion is based on fear of the prince. Whatever the reason, the omission is not entirely necessary for the plot or structure of the story. Callirhoe's retelling of the whole story reinforced the individual episodes of her adventures on the reader (audience) and emphasized the oral flavor, which Chariton seemed to favor.

Before dismissing her, Dionysius consoled Callirhoe and promised to help her, even though he recognized that Eros or Aphrodite was toying with him and torturing his libido, already in a shattered state because of the death of his wife.

Curiously, Dionysius mentioned to Leonas that he has come to think of Callirhoe as a gift from Aphrodite, much as Helen had been for Menelaus. This is another analogue from myth, of which Chariton is so fond, and it adds a foreboding note of impending trouble. Helen had started a war; what could Callirhoe do? Because he now believed Callirhoe lost to him, Dionysius sank to such a low point that he swore to kill himself when she returned to her home and left Miletus. Suicide was another often repeated motif by Chariton who surely stressed the theatrical.

A penetrating look both into the workings of, and differences in, the prince's character and that of his chief steward Leonas is offered by the exchange between the two, immediately after Dionysius threatened suicide. Leonas felt that as lord and master of Miletus, Dionysius could force Callirhoe to bend to his will; furthermore, he owned her by right of purchase from Theron. The prince would have none of it and in fact turned on his chief steward and rebuked him in the strongest language. Though he cited many reasons for freeing his newest "slave," the compelling reasons for freedom all had to do with the nature of his own moral character: it was not so much that Callirhoe *deserved* to be sent back to Syracuse; rather it was consistent with the high ethical standards he had set for himself. But Leonas did not understand Dionysius, and it was now obvious that Dionysius had not had much influence on the amoral Leonas. The steward was not his own man; he tried to anticipate the moves of his superiors and in this case (also in others), he misjudged them. The contrast of master and steward drawn by Chariton is excellent. Neither character is a mere foil to the other.

Another of Dionysius's servants who had some of her master's interests at heart and who, like Leonas, tried to please him without considering his best interests, was Plangon, wife of Phocas, and special attendant to Callirhoe. Plangon worked in her own way for Dionysius, never forgetting to watch out for herself and her husband, but her special area of competence was trickery. When Dionysius entrusted Callirhoe to her, Plangon believed that she had also been ordered to convince Callirhoe to marry him. Dionysius never intended that his words have such a nuance. But this servant, like others in Chariton and like very many in Greek New Comedy, was a trickster who frequently aided her master in all the wrong ways, namely by believing that her master had all the baser instincts that she had.

We believe that this episode, involving the tricks of a slave, represents a motif from Greek New Comedy and Roman comedy which became a standard pose for slaves in imaginative literature. To carry out her plan, which she believed to be consistent with Dionysius's wishes, Plangon seized on a chance remark of his about her husband and fabricated a story for Callirhoe: she claimed that Dionysius was so displeased with her husband, Phocas, that he was considering doing away with him. Plangon begged Callirhoe to intercede on their behalf with the prince, confirming that the prince would listen to a noblewoman like her. As Callirhoe presented her pleas for pardon of Phocas, Dionysius recognized what Plangon has been doing and planning, and he followed her lead. He pardoned both Phocas and Plangon, pointing out to Callirhoe that he was sparing them only on her account. Callirhoe was simply overwhelmed, and as she embraced Plangon, she was pushed forward by the latter toward Dionysius, who caught her and stole a kiss before releasing her. Callirhoe left, but Dionysius was now totally committed to loving her. His only avenue of approach to her now was the slave Plangon, to whom he offered freedom as a prize in return for helping him win Callirhoe.

One of the most interesting twists in the plot is disclosed at this point. It is brought about by Fortune, "who loves to do the unexpected, to act in a contrary fashion. And on this occasion she effects a situation which surprises everyone. The means she used are worthy of hearing." Chariton stepped forward here and announced that he was going to relate something special, something the reader would want to hear. This address to the reader was used sparingly by Chariton, and then only when he wanted to attract special attention to something. This was probably parallel to an actor's aside to the audience in a drama. The scene he wished to describe was one suitable for drama and the stage—in fact, part of the scene came from a play of Euripides.

Now two months after her marriage to Chaereas, Callirhoe

discovered that she was pregnant with his child. Plangon also had observed the slight swelling in her belly and suspected what Callirhoe then confessed. The reaction of the two women revealed clearly the difference in their characters. Plangon saw the unborn child as an ally in bringing about some kind of union between Callirhoe and Dionysius. Such a union would mean her freedom. Callirhoe, on the other hand, wanted no marriage partner other than Chaereas, and since she believed that the child would be born in Asia (not Greece), in slavery (not freedom), and far from her family, she was determined to have an abortion. This plan of Callirhoe was not so radical in the ancient world as we might think. While the later part of our century is experiencing a kind of sexual revolution, the ancient world required no such revolution to make abortion a standard practice of escaping from an otherwise ugly situation.[7] In a soliloquy similar to Medea's (Euripides *Medea* 1019 ff.), Callirhoe lamented her fate and that of her unborn child. How much better it would be if the child would die before knowing slavery or hearing the terrible stories of his noble mother reduced to the status of a servant. In answer to her own soliloquy Chariton had Callirhoe take the speaking part of her own child and plead for his life:

"Are you really a Medea and is a Jason outraging you so that you will resort to actions similar to Medea's? What if he is a boy, and looks just like his father? There is every possibility he can live a happier life than you ... [then in a prophetic mood] someday my child will sail back to Syracuse and tell his father and grandfather all about his mother's experiences. My son together with a fleet will rescue me and reunite his father and me."

The analogue from myth is particularly graphic, for the reader was meant to see Callirhoe as a type of Medea, murderer of her children. The fact that Callirhoe does not go through with the threatened abortion probably reflected on the middle-class morality transferred from Chariton to the aristocratic expectant mother. The last two sentences in the above quote contain information that only Chariton and the reader should know. There was no way for Callirhoe to have guessed the denouement of this adventure story. It is reasonable to suggest that Callirhoe is revealing the outcome of the story to the reader, but does not herself understand the full import of what she was saying. Perhaps Chariton saw it as a kind of "inner aside" to the audience. Regardless of our interpretation of what is obviously out of place, Chariton was surely trying to hint at the final results of the plot and keep the reader informed to a much fuller degree than the characters. Chariton viewed his novel as a type of drama in which the playwright and audience know the full story, while the actors stumble into trouble. It was his favorite kind of irony. When Callirhoe finally went to sleep, she dreamed of her husband who said that he was placing the sole care of their son into her hands.

Plangon now began a cat-and-mouse game with Callirhoe, in which she urged her to have an abortion but said it in such a way that the opposite course of raising the child was always more appealing. By delaying day after day and throwing the dilemma at the distraught Callirhoe, Plangon was playing tricks for which slaves were famous. Chariton again moved back to a familiar motif. Finally, Callirhoe chose the easier of the two alternatives, the one in which she was the passive agent rather than the active: she would submit to a marriage with Dionysius. An aristocratic princess would have chosen suicide for herself and death for her foetus, but she did not have the bearing of an aristocrat. Callirhoe had only one final fear: that Dionysius might suspect the child was not his. But Plangon assured her that since she was only two months pregnant she could fool Dionysius into believing he had fathered a premature baby. In antiquity there was an often repeated maxim that you could always tell who was the mother of the child but not who his father was. In the *Odyssey* (1.213ff.), for instance, Telemachus says that he knows his mother but that it is only from reports that he has head that Odysseus is his father. Apparently this proverbial expression became a kind of motif which Chariton picked up and used here. Plautus also employed it in his comedy *Amphitryo* (195 B.C.).

V   *Act I (Book 3-3.2): Marriage or Bigamy*

Only the first two chapters of the third book belong to Act I of Chariton's drama. Beginning with the third chapter Chariton went back to Syracuse to pick up the thread of the story concerning our hero, Chaereas, who had been left standing at Callirhoe's empty tomb. The content of the first book was largely marked by action; the second book was free of action and concentrated on psychological exploration on a relatively peaceful scene; the third book returns to action. Chariton was obviously alternating two kinds of approaches and trying to establish a tempo. Though both contained a built-in level of tension, the alternation of action and calm provided the reader with partial relief from what went on earlier. At the same time, as we see Plangon victorious over Callirhoe and Callirhoe resigned to take another husband (as far as she knows Chaereas was alive and this presented her with a certain moral problem), we are given a picture of Dionysius as a man bent on suicide, preparing his will.

As only a coarse slave can do, Plangon rushed to his rooms and blurted out that Callirhoe wanted to marry him at once. He fainted on the spot—not in the manner of a true-to-life despot but like a sentimental, middle-class peasant. The description of Dionysius passing out was almost a word for word verbal parallel with Callirhoe's fainting on hearing that Chaereas wanted to marry her (1.1). The phrases, which are all but identical, imitate Homer's epic descriptions and were employed by Chariton as *formulae*. The reader was obviously meant to associate the second use of the *formula* here with the first. Dionysius's fainting spell was so severe that he appeared dead to all those around him. Word quickly ran through the palace that Dionysius had died, and all, including Callirhoe, mourned him. Like Lazarus, however, he arose from the dead. Chariton was clearly attracted to the scheme of apparent death-resurrection: both Callirhoe and Dionysius fainted and appeared dead; Callirhoe was kicked, seemingly died, and was in fact buried. But none of them die. Chariton used this motif sparingly but in later writers, especially Heliodorus and Achilles Tatius, apparent death-resurrection scenes are employed to a ridiculous degree. Perhaps Chariton started the tradition of such episodes, which brought a kind of dramatic tension to the story and allowed the writer to spend some time luxuriating in the emotion of that moment of death.

Dionysius quickly recovered and was assured by Plangon that he was not dreaming and Callirhoe still wished to marry him. The prince was ecstatic and acted like one of the young lovers (either free or slave) which we have learned to know in Greek and Roman comedy:

"Tell me what she said, exactly, in her own words. Do not leave any iota out, do not put in anything extra. Let me have her words verbatim."

The audience or reader was never given Callirhoe's words verbatim, so that we must rely on what Plangon said they were. Callirhoe had consented to marry Dionysius, but she would hang herself if he wanted her only as a mistress. In her short speech to Dionysius, Plangon sandwiched in a clever condition:

"Think this marriage proposal over seriously with your advisors so that after you are married and have a child no one will ask you: 'Are you, a prince, going to raise children which you fathered with a slave?' She told me to tell you that if you do not want to be a father, you will never be her husband."

Dionysius was so much in love with her body (and so, as the physionomicists argue, also with her character and soul) that he did not question the condition of being a father to her child. Of course Dionysius knew nothing of Callirhoe's first marriage or that she was at present two months pregnant. This was a real blemish on the otherwise spotless character of Callirhoe. Her deceit would haunt her for some time and force her later to be separated from someone she loved dearly. The prime mover of the deceit, Plangon, could be excused primarily on the grounds that she was a slave (and so thought like a slave), and secondly, because this deceit would result in her own freedom. The irony of the situation was brought off well, and the superior position of the reader reflected the irony of a good Greek tragedy. Callirhoe further asked Dionysius to swear before the gods that he would treat her kindly forever because, she added, "A lonely woman in a foreign land is at the mercy of all."

It is one of the memorable lines from Chariton's pen. He swore his oath before Eros and Aphrodite, the latter being Callirhoe's patron saint. In order to ward off all suspicion about whether or not Callirhoe was a slave and to guard himself against possible actions from Hermocrates for mistreating her or forcing her against her will, Dionysius decided to marry her at a public ceremony in Miletus and provided a banquet for the entire city.

Before she left for Miletus, Callirhoe entered the temple of Aphrodite to pray that her deceit would go undetected. Callirhoe had developed a certain ambivalence toward Aphrodite because this deity was both her bane and her balm. Aphrodite, in one aspect of her nature, which was kindly, helped lovers to find each other. In another aspect, which was mysteriously violent, cruel, and animalistic, she drove lovers apart and into someone else's arms. Callirhoe visited the temple also because she was already feeling the first real pangs of conscience now that Dionysius has accepted, set the date, and was preparing the wedding bed. She had betrayed Chaereas and deceived Dionysius.

The first act closes as Chariton steps forward and addresses the audience:

Again, and even on this day, that demon, Envy, strikes out. The way all this happens I will tell just a little later, but right now I want to tell you what has been happening in the meantime in Syracuse.

Chariton did not want, or perhaps he was unable, to blend together the two plots which have now formed. We see here that just as stability and happiness returned to the life of Callirhoe, so did the demon Envy. When Callirhoe was happy and about to be the princess of Miletus, the gods became jealous and struck her down. At her first marriage we saw the same thing, where Envy (*phthonos*; here *daimon baskanos*) visited terrible punishment on the new bride. This theme of envious gods destroying the lives of seemingly favored humans stands clearly within the best traditions of Greek literature and history, and in a small way illustrates Chariton's affinity to that tradition.

Callirhoe's second marriage, which was bigamy even in Chariton's time, placed a special tension on the plot. Though the dominant motif in this novel, as in the other four Greek works of the same genre, was erotic, and we are never allowed to forget that Callirhoe and Chaereas were constantly and in all places in their travels deeply in love with each other, there was a premium (outside of love and eroticism) placed on virtue and chastity. All the other heroines (as usual there is a different standard for heroes) in the remaining Greek novels remained chaste and preserved their virginity. Anthia in Xenophon of Ephesus's novel, like Callirhoe, married and then was separated from her husband. But she had nothing to do with other men. Chariclea in Heliodorus, Chloe in Longus, and Leucippe in Achilles Tatius, all met and were separated before they married. But each of these three remained a virgin until she married her betrothed. Thus it is that only Callirhoe was unfaithful to her husband.

It remains a possibility to argue that Callirhoe married Dionysius because she thought Chaereas was dead.[8] She cannot, however, be defended on this ground, because she did not know for certain that Chaereas was dead until Phocas told her (end of Bk. 3). According to the time sequence of the plot, Callirhoe married Chaereas first, Dionysius second; seven months later she had her baby; shortly thereafter she learned from Phocas that Chaereas had been killed. In comparison with the other incredibly virtuous heroines of Greek romance, it is worthwhile to note that Callirhoe was not as virtuous as the rest. Apparently the standard of conduct for heroines in this genre was absolute chastity. Callirhoe was too human and real for such a high level of morality. Chariton obviously desired to make his heroine a three-dimensional character, though he realized that such a deviation in delineation of character types ran counter to the regular or accepted form. A look at the other heroines in Greek romance show the reader that the character or *persona* of Callirhoe as drawn by Chariton was superior. She had the usual virtuous side to her nature, but she also had the darker side which leaned toward sex without love. She had the usual strength of romantic heroines, but also an unexpected and quite human weakness. Then too, in her future relations with Dionysius and Chaereas, her act of faithlessness developed an all-around tension in the story which is not to be found in the other Greek novels.

CHAPTER 5

A Happy Ending

I *Act II (Book 3.3-4): Bad Times for Pirates and Heroes*

AFTER Callirhoe's relatives and husband had sealed her tomb and returned home, Chariton did not mention any of them again until chapter three of the third book. To this point the adventures of Callirhoe dominated absolutely. Now Chariton retraced his steps and discussed all unfinished business in reverse chronological order: the last person from Syracuse to see Callirhoe and also her connecting link to that city was Theron, who was discussed first. Continuing backward in time, Chariton next related the adventures of Chaereas who saw Callirhoe just before Theron stole her from the tomb.

In their haste to escape the scene of the crime, the grave robbers had not resealed the tomb, whose open door greeted Chaereas as he came early in the morning on the day after the funeral. He had come to kill himself. His close inspection revealed that not only had the grave robbers got the gold but the corpse was also missing. It is evident that had the pirates not taken Callirhoe with them, Chaereas would have killed himself before ascertaining if she were alive. After all who looks for life in a tomb? The scene would thus have imitated Sophocles' *Antigone* and foreshadowed *Romeo and Juliet*. On reaching the empty tomb Chaereas first suspected that the gods had become so jealous of him that they had stolen her, as Dionysus had stolen Ariadne. The mythic analogue, as mentioned already, here makes Callirhoe a type of the stolen Ariadne (stolen bride). Casting about, Chaereas next wondered if his bride might not have been a goddess come to earth, who after a short time had to return to the home of the gods. Lastly, he grasped some measure of reality and realized that she had been stolen by grave robbers along with the gold. If this was true, it followed

104

that she was still alive. Searchers ran off in all directions to discover what happened to Callirhoe, but it was Fortune, said Chariton, who could explain the disappearance of Callirhoe.

After the pirates had sold Callirhoe in Miletus, they set sail for Crete but were driven past it into the Ionian Sea between Greece and Italy. There we see them on board ship, lying ill and dying of thirst because the winds were unfavorable and provisions had run out:

Fate illustrated to the pirates that they had sailed earlier in fair weather because Callirhoe was with them on the ship. Nor were they allowed to die mercifully or quickly; even the dry land refused to welcome such wicked men. In the midst of a hoard of gold and riches the pirates were dying from a lack of fresh water—an extremely cheap commodity to good people. Among these villains Theron remained the most villainous: he stole water from his comrades and so lived while all the others died.

Chariton was very fond of contrasts, and the above paragraph illustrates it nicely. The sea was for villains and the dry land was for the innocent. This was perhaps a natural sentiment for a man from the interior of Asia Minor. His contrast of riches, for which all strive but do not necessarily need, and water, which all need but normally do not strive for, is the simplistic kind of moral equation, like black and white, which we see Chariton make quite frequently. A contrast which dominates all others and which illustrates Chariton's approach (feeling) toward his characters is that of innocence-guilt. Guilty persons are awarded retribution in proportion to their crime, while innocent people, though buffeted by Fate, find a happy ending. Thus the punishment of Theron is more severe than that meted out to his comrades, because he was the instigator of the crime.

In his search for Callirhoe, Chaereas came upon Theron's derelict ship, found all the treasure from his bride's tomb, and rescued Theron, who was unknown to Chaereas, from certain death. His capture here was a kind of *deus ex machina*. Theron, who never lost his balance, no matter how bad the situation became, claimed to be a passenger on board, who was spared by the gods because of his piety. Back in Syracuse Hermocrates and others prepared an inquest to learn the facts in the case.

This scene was made for Chariton: he described the weeping and wailing, tearing of hair, beating of breasts. The people were lost in sorrow because Callirhoe was now surely lost. Again Chariton luxuriated everywhere in unrestrained emotions. After Chaereas had told how he found the ship and Callirhoe's funeral equipment, Theron was brought forward in chains, followed by the wheel, the rack, fire, and whips. These are ominous signs —especially to an audience who recognized them. Theron claimed that his name was Demetrius and that he had been only a passenger on the boat from Crete and had not known that his comrades were pirates. The assembled crowd like the chorus in Greek tragedy sympathized with him. But a certain fisherman in the crowd testified that, prior to Callirhoe's burial, he had seen Theron in the harbor area of Syracuse. The sympathies of the crowd quickly turned againt Theron, and he was ordered tortured until he told the whole truth. Theron did not go over the whole story, which we have heard at least twice before, but he filled in only that information which the audience (not the reader) and the principals, Chaereas and Hermocrates, could not know. Such restraint at this point in not retelling the whole story again illustrates that Chariton has firm control of his characters and their actions. In the Greek novels this kind of restraint was not customary.

For the first time now there was hope in Chaereas's heart that, even though Callirhoe had been sold into slavery, he would find her alive. Theron had admitted selling her in Miletus, but Hermocrates did not feel it was safe to allow Theron to accompany Chaereas there to point out her buyers. Instead, Theron was impaled on a pike in front of Callirhoe's tomb. The punishment of Theron is particularly gruesome and unparalleled in the remainder of the book. The Greek word here for "to impale" is marvelously graphic, *anaskolopizein*. The image behind the word is "to skewer," "to fix on a pole." That fine Greek spirit which we think of as striving for all things beautiful obviously had a darker side. Throughout the episodes in which he had taken part, Theron had never been painted as a real villain. He robbed Callirhoe's tomb, but in so doing, probably saved her from certain death by starvation. Rather than kill her, he sold her in Miletus. As his fellow pirates lay dying of thirst, he did steal extra portions of water. This was hardly a villainous act. In view of this, the punishment does not fit the crime. Perhaps it is intended that we see the tortures inflicted on Theron to make him tell the truth as a type of ordeal, which Theron could not pass or go through because of an evil flaw in him, not articulated by Chariton.

Here in Book 3.4 with the death of Theron we have a major turning point. Theron to this time had been the dominant male figure, but he had failed his ordeal. Chaereas now begins his ordeal, which will not end until the novel does. In a steadily rising crescendo Chaereas makes his voice and authority heard above those of his friends and enemies, and at the conclusion of the story will pass through the final ordeal and take his place among other Greek heroes like Hermocrates, his father-in-law, to whom he is constantly compared (as equal) or contrasted (as a lesser being). In Heliodorus and Achilles Tatius heroes were subjected to different kinds of ordeals, namely ordeals to test and prove or disprove chastity. The ordeals in Chariton stressed manliness and the qualities we associate with heroes. We should expect this because Chariton was writing of characters who look back toward, and find precedents in, earlier Greek history, epic, and drama. Later Greek novelists turned away from heroes of action to passive heroes of love. Ordeals of valor yielded to ordeals of chastity. The man of heroic reputation was later not as important as the hero with a reputation as a virgin.

Chaereas prepared to set sail immediately for Miletus, and the city government of Syracuse agreed to pay for the expeditionary expenses. The parents of Chaereas tried to force him to delay sailing because of the rough winter seas. He was so torn between Callirhoe and his parents' wishes that he attempted one of his many suicides. The unrestrained and uncritical suicide attempts at every turn of ill-fortune, plus the immediate despair in difficult situations, show clearly that just below the surface of reality lay a well of emotions. If reality was scratched even in the slightest, the emotions welled up and spilled over. Chariton did not expect, nor would he have got it had he expected it, intellectual judgment from his audience. He realized from beginning to end that his readers were happiest with a sentimental work.

Both Chaereas and his double Polycharmus set sail for Miletus in the face of their parents' pleas and an outpouring of sentimentality: "The whole town exploded with prayers, tears, moans, encouraging shouts, fear, courage, despair, and hope." The journey of Chaereas, his departure from his home, the act of leaving or deserting his parents, all these were calculated to appeal to the emotions of the middle-class audience. In defense of Chariton there are many early classical precedents of such emotional leave-taking scenes: quickly to mind come Dido's farewell to Aeneas; Laodamia's good-bye to Protesilaus; Hero and Leander; Circe and Odysseus; and Aegeus and his son Theseus.

Chaereas's ship followed in the tracks, as it were, of Theron and arrived at the same country estate of Dionysius, where our heroes visited the temple of Aphrodite. There they saw a statue of Callirhoe before which Chaereas fainted (in the exact words of Callirhoe's and Dionysius's faint—a *formula*). After learning that Callirhoe has become Dionysius's princess, Chaereas breaks into one of his frequent soliloquies of despair. This one, however, displays a little of Chariton's humor:

"Though many bad things have happened to me, I never expected Callirhoe to marry again—not even after I had died. . . . Then if she had only married someone whose station was below mine, I could have rescued her. But how can I buy her back from a man who has more money than I have. If I approach her I could be put to death as an adulterer of mine own wife!"

Such a contrived plot as the love triangle of Chaereas-Callirhoe-Dionysius is what the ancient rhetoricans called a *controversia,* an imaginary situation, which is frequently a lawsuit, but which can be argued well on both sides. A *controversia* is really a rhetorical exercise and a fabricated case which young law students can argue about for practice. It is roughly like the cases in our moot court. An example of a *controversia* from antiquity is this: "The punishment for rape is that the woman may demand the man's death or make him marry her. A man raped two women in one night. The first wants him executed; second wants to marry him."[1]

For the first time in this novel the story-plot now becomes

complicated, and we realize that Chariton has set several forces into action at the same time. After Chaereas's ship docked, Phocas, one of Dionysius's trusted servants, inquired about the strangers and learned their identity. Realizing the danger for Dionysius and ultimately for himself, Phocas recruited some barbarians (i.e., non-Greeks) to destroy the ship and its sailors. Chaereas and Polycharmus are caught and sold as slaves in Caria (southwest Asia Minor). Dionysius meanwhile had learned all about Chaereas from Callirhoe, caught talking in her sleep. Like dreams, talking in one's sleep was always regarded as the truth being exposed through the agency of a deity. This shock for Dionysius, however, was set aside at the birth of *his* son. For the time being Callirhoe also put the matter of her former husband out of her mind.

To insure that Plangon did not disclose the real father of Callirhoe's son to Dionysius, Callirhoe begged the prince to set Plangon free. This is only one of the many requests Dionysius granted Callirhoe, as he reveled in the thought of having had a child by her. Thank offerings were made to Aphrodite, and the whole household of the prince made a pilgrimage to her temple. After Dionysius had made a public offering to Aphrodite, Callirhoe and Plangon went privately into the temple and prayed:

"Though you have not given Chaereas back to me, I thank you for having given me a mirror image of him in my young son. . . . Perhaps someday people will say that he is a greater man than Hermocrates was."

After this Callirhoe broke down, cried, and rehearsed all her past bad experiences. It appears here that Chariton is again thinking of Callirhoe's son as the famous Dionysius I, tyrant of Syracuse. (The tyrant was in reality Hermocrates' son-in-law, not his grandson.)

At the temple the priestess of Aphrodite told Callirhoe about the visit of a man who fit the description of Chaereas. Because Callirhoe knew Dionysius was jealous and would investigate the matter, she mentioned the priestess's discussion of Chaereas to him. Suspecting a plot at his country estate, Dionysius threatened everyone with torture, but Phocas admitted he knew all the facts in the case and related them to Dionysius before anyone was hurt:

"It is really nothing serious, master. In the beginning it sounds bad, but do not worry. Wait until you hear the outcome. It ends well for you. A warship came here from Syracuse and demanded that we give back Callirhoe."

Dionysius, who seemed disposed to such acts, fainted again, and the fainting is once more described in the same words as the three earlier faintings (i.e., by the *formula*). This speech of Phocas to Dionysius, in which he told him not to worry about the first events but to trust that all would turn out well for him, was taken almost directly from the repertory of tricks played on masters by the servants in Greek New Comedy and Latin comedy: slaves first report the bad news, enjoy their masters' suffering, and then report the good. Dionysius soon revived and learned that the ship on which Chaereas had sailed and many of the hands were lost. His thanks to Phocas showed that he had practical understanding of situation ethics:

"You are a great and faithful servant. Because of you I still have my Callirhoe. While *I* would never have had Chaereas killed, I do not criticize you for having done it. It was merely the honest crime of a faithful servant. If there is any blame attached to you in this whole affair, it is a matter of negligence that you did not find out for certain if Chaereas was one of the dead."

Hiding from Callirhoe the facts that Phocas instigated the attack on Chaereas's ship and that it was not certain he was dead, Dionysius had eyewitnesses tell her about the destruction of the ship. In a long tirade Callirhoe accused Aphrodite of bringing about Chaereas's death and then indulged in an emotional outburst of pity for her baby, her husband, and herself.

II   *Act II (Book 4): Callirhoe Finds Several New Lovers*

Excitement apart from action in the plot continued to grow throughout the fourth book, and it is apparent that the increasing complications are leading rapidly toward a highly unstable situation which must be resolved in some way.

To change the mood of Callirhoe and to remove Chaereas from her every thought, Dionysius suggested to her that she build a tomb for Chaereas. The constant reminder of the tomb would hopefully reinforce the idea that Chaereas was dead. Once hope for him was lost, she would no longer think of him. Dionysius persuaded her not to build the tomb near the temple of Aphrodite (he associated himself and his recent marriage with that temple) but in the city of Miletus where many people could see it. The funeral memorial was well attended and even Mithridates, governor of Caria, and Pharnaces, governor of Lydia, put in personal appearances. The picture of a grieving widow following a long and richly decorated funeral procession was used frequently by earlier classical writers (e.g., Petronius's "Widow of Ephesus") and also by those who followed Chariton. As Mithridates, royal governor of Caria, had his first glimpse of Callirhoe, he also fainted. Chariton continued to play with ironic situations but sometimes his contrivances were too cute. Consider Callirhoe's speech at Chaereas's tomb:

"You first buried me in Syracuse, and now I am burying you in Miletus. . . . We have now buried each other but neither one of us has the body of the other before which to pay proper respects."

Meanwhile, Chaereas and Polycharmus were working on a slave chain gang in Caria. But because Chaereas was too sick from worry over Callirhoe, faithful (every epic hero had a faithful friend) Polycharmus was doing the work of two men. Like Chaereas, Mithridates was described by Chariton as also wasting away for love and appearing thin and pale, like all good lovers. A prison break occurred in Chaereas's cell, and an overseer was killed, an act which caused the governor Mithridates to condemn all the men in that cell, even the innocent Chaereas and Polycharmus, to be crucified. As preparations for the crucifixion were carried out, Polycharmus cursed Callirhoe as the source of all their troubles. The head of the crucifixion squad, believing someone named Callirhoe was also in on the prison escape, took Polycharmus before Mithridates to learn what role she had played. After a proper amount of torture, Polycharmus confessed the whole story of Chaereas and Callirhoe and his part in it. Mithridates, of course, was already familiar with certain aspects of the case because he had attended Chaereas's memorial funeral. The order went out immediately to save Chaereas as he was about to mount the cross. Instead of rejoicing at his deliverance or fainting as others had done, Chaereas was sad and dejected because he was determined to die. He no longer had any desire to live. He exhibited the kind of pessimism we discussed in the second chapter above. His pessimism and apparently wasted existence could have been finally redeemed by love through death on the cross. From Mithridates Chaereas learned that Callirhoe has remarried and has had a child:

"Faithless Callirhoe, most wicked of women! Was I sold into slavery for your sake!"

The irony of the above passage becomes clear, if we recall that Callirhoe earlier lamented Chaereas's act of burying her quickly, which resulted in her being sold into slavery. The same night that Chaereas was rescued, we find Mithridates unable to sleep, plotting how he could best set Chaereas against Dionysius, and then how he might move in and steal the prize. The next morning Chaereas asked to be allowed to go to Miletus to fetch Callirhoe, but was advised by the governor not to go:

"If I thought it were good for you to go, I would aid you myself. . . . But fortune has given you a terrible role in a melancholy drama, and you must take care of your life. . . . You have had bad experiences up until now, and if you go to Miletus, I will not be able to protect you. . . . Do you seriously think Dionysius will surrender his wife to you just because you want her? . . . I suggest that instead of traveling to Miletus, you send her a letter, and I will see to it that it gets there."

Chaereas composed a letter full of self-pity and pleaded with Callirhoe to return to him, her legitimate husband. This letter, along with a personal note for Callirhoe from Mithridates, was entrusted to Hyginus, who was to take along three slaves with mounds of gold for presents. The slaves, who were told that the gold was for the satrap Dionysius, were left with the gold in Priene while Hyginus went alone to scout out the situation in Miletus. Left without direction in Priene, the slaves began to squander the gold, attracted the attention of the busybody Greeks and even of the mayor, Bias, and were finally arrested as thieves. Chariton again makes a kind of racial slur about the inquisitiveness of the Greeks who were constantly interfering with the business of other people and confusing their plans.

Having received from Bias the slaves' gold (the slaves had told Bias all they knew: the gold was for Dionysius) and the unopened letters, Dionysius fainted dead away, again described in the exact same words as his and Callirhoe's earlier collapses. Dionysius kept the letters to himself and brought charges of attempted wife-stealing against Mithridates before Pharnaces, governor of Lydia and enemy of Mithridates. Lydia was on the immediate northern boundary of Caria, and their two governors were rivals. Pharnaces had another reason for coming to the aid of Dionysius: he also had seen Callirhoe at Chaereas's memorial funeral and was now in love with her. So Pharnaces wrote to Artaxerxes, king of all Persia and surrounding lands, to ask his help in dealing with this immoral conduct of one of his highest ranking officials. Chariton was obviously a student of political systems because he carefully traced the appeals of Dionysius through the proper administrative channels. Artaxerxes was not particularly pleased to have to deal with such a thorny problem, but he (like so many others!) was especially eager to get a look at this international beauty named Callirhoe. And so Artaxerxes was added to the list of Callirhoe's suitors: Chaereas, Dionysius, Mithridates, Pharnaces, and now Artaxerxes. The list of suitors is almost as long as it was in the beginning of the novel, when all the young men were eager to catch Callirhoe, and the prize fell to Chaereas.

All interested parties were ordered to Babylon, Artaxerxes's capital, for trial. After Mithridates learned from Hyginus what had gone wrong in Miletus, he hesitated (in fact, he thought of revolting) to go to Babylon, but then started out anyway when he heard that Dionysius and Callirhoe were already on their way. Now Dionysius began to have second thoughts about his quest for justice. It occurred to him that Pharnaces and

Artaxerxes might be helping him only to get an opportunity to
try to steal his Callirhoe.

III   *Act III* (*Books 5-6*): *Trial by Jury or Justice and Love Are Blind*

The fifth book opens with a brief summary of the first four
books, and Chariton in the role of the author promises at this
point to tie up the strings that bind the earlier episodes with
the conclusion. Though Callirhoe had severed her connections
with the many things Greek when she decided to marry Dionysius, her biggest break with her former life occurred here when
she crossed the Euphrates River, which Callirhoe clearly indicated was a barrier between things Greek in the West and
things Persian in the East. Now that she no longer saw the sea,
she completely lost all orientation and sense of belonging. While
she lived at Miletus she had known that a common sea connected
her to Greece and further to Syracuse. She expressed the same
feeling of loneliness and isolation, which set in now that she was
distant from the sea, much as Xenophon of Athens and his men
felt in their *Anabasis* into Asia Minor to fight as mercenaries for
Cyrus. For most Greeks of this time the sea apparently functioned as a kind of "security blanket."

Callirhoe cursed cruel Fortune, kissed the ground on the
west side of the Euphrates, and there boarded a ferry for the
other side. Her action in kissing the ground marked a clearly
defined line of separation between one life and another, between
one kind of world and another. Callirhoe was obviously on a
journey, but perhaps this trip to Babylon was only an outward
symbol for her more important journey through life—from the
uninitiated virgin of Syracuse to the mother and guiding spirit
of the future ruler of Syracuse who blessed her son with her
wisdom and experience. It was necessary therefore for her to
have left Syracuse. Though he did not talk about Greek novels,
Joseph Campbell finds this kind of symbolic journey in many
literatures:

As we soon . . . see, whether presented in the vast, almost oceanic
images of the Orient, in the vigorous narratives of the Greeks, or

in the majestic legends of the Bible, the adventure of the hero normally follows the pattern: a separation from the world, a penetration to some source of power, and a life-enhancing return.[2]

While the regal procession of Dionysius and Callirhoe made its way to Babylon, Mithridates and Chaereas hurried to arrive and present their side of the case first. Introduced by Artaxates, King Artaxerxes's eunuch and chief advisor, Mithridates was, however, dismissed until Dionysius arrived. Rebuffed in this scheme, Mithridates plotted courtroom strategy with Chaereas and told him to remain in hiding in the courtroom and not to come out until called, no matter what the situation was. Mithridates told Chaereas that this was the only favor he would ask in return for his help in securing Callirhoe. Chaereas, however, bemoaned his fate which would not allow him to embrace Callirhoe though they were so close. Dionysius meanwhile had his hands full keeping sight-seers away from Callirhoe. Chariton (in his anti-Persian way) claimed that the beautiful wife of Dionysius was crushed by crowds because "barbarians are by nature madly romantic."

Dionysius grew more and more apprehensive as they approached Babylon and the risky business of exposing Callirhoe to the gaze of many powerful men:

"Why did I bring Callirhoe to Babylon, a city full of men like Mithridates! I should have remembered that even in puritanical and conservative Sparta Menelaus could not guard Helen's bedroom door. A barbarian from Asia got to her. Just consider how many men like Paris there are among the Persians!"

All these rumors of the beautiful Callirhoe have now aroused the jealousy of the Persian women, who sent out the most beautiful Persian woman, Rhodogyne, to meet Dionysius and to embarrass and shame his wife. As Rhodogyne waited to welcome Callirhoe at the city's gates, Chariton described her as a woman dressed and set for a contest, a royal beauty prepared to challenge this foreign woman and rival. To avoid the peering eyes of the crowds along the way, Dionysius had drawn the curtains on Callirhoe's carriage, but was forced to open them and expose her now that they had been confronted by a royal welcoming committee.

In this contest, which Chariton has so carefully constructed, Callirhoe emerged in an instant as the victor. She had entered upon her ordeal with the best, the champion, the beauty chosen by the Persian women themselves, and now she emerged from the ordeal as the most beautiful woman in Greece and Persia. The Persians standing at the scene declared her the winner.

After delaying the trial for thirty days on religious grounds, Artaxerxes ordered the trial to begin. "Which of the Olympic Games ever held such suspense?" asked Chariton. With Artaxerxes presiding, the trial began; the letters of Chaereas and Mithridates were read first, and Dionysius, as plaintiff, was asked to present his opening and closing arguments. Mithridates, however, objected to conducting this trial without having the cause of all the trouble, Callirhoe, present. Heated arguments followed on both sides, Mithridates because he wanted to see Callirhoe, if only in court, Dionysius because he had not yet told his wife why they had made the long journey to Babylon. Because of the dispute the king ordered a recess, and Callirhoe learned the whole truth for the first time. During the following night she dreamed that she was back in Syracuse in the temple of Aphrodite, preparing to marry Chaereas, a propitious dream meant to encourage Callirhoe (and the reader) that all would turn out well in the end. Chariton made full use of the motif of the prophetic dreams, but he also perhaps used it too often. His employment of dreams established a tension between the present and frightening reality of the future with its promises for a better life. When Chariton wished to discourage certain actions of a character, he had him dream a foreboding dream; sometimes the dreams were apparently meant more for the readers than the players.

What followed now in the courtroom was Chariton's tour de force. He brought to bear on the speeches of Dionysius and Mithridates in the courtroom all the rhetorical expertise of which he was capable; he went to the bottom of the well of his education and ability and produced a drama (his own word) worthy of the Silver Age of Greek literature. Chariton followed the best Greek rhetorical form of his time and had Dionysius and Mithridates present the king (and the reader) with a perfect (rhetorically speaking) example of what was called *iudicale genus dicendi* (law court speech). Each speaker followed the established outline: *exordium, narratio, probatio, conclusio.*

SPEECH AND CHARGES OF DIONYSIUS

Exordium (Introduction):

The crime of Mithridates was of the worst kind because, though he was a guest friend of his, he tried to steal his wife. Artaxerxes must punish Mithridates, the governor, for his actions because they reflected poorly on the great king.

Narratio (Case History):

Dionysius claimed that Mithridates fell in love with his wife when he visited them at the occasion of the ceremonial funeral for Chaereas.

Probatio (Evidence):

Bias was a witness to Mithridates's crime and the great king had seen the letters of Mithridates, which Mithridates claimed Chaereas wrote.

Conclusio (Summary):

It is obvious that Mithridates was guilty, for all the evidence pointed that way. He was a would-be adulterer who, by claiming to have raised Chaereas from the dead, dishonored his name.

SPEECH AND REBUTTAL OF MITHRIDATES

Exordium:

Mithridates claimed he had in the past always been a good governor and served the king well. These accusations of Dionysius were nothing but slander. Who would prefer the love of Callirhoe to the respect of the great king? How could Dionysius bring charges of adultery against anyone, when he bought his wife as a slave and did not even have her registration papers?

Narratio:

After rehearsing the whole case for the Persian court (a case the reader knew), Mithridates did not try to defend himself but rather brought countercharges of adultery against Dionysius. In fact, Mithridates pleaded with his opponent to withdraw his charges before it was too late, and he was convicted of adultery.

Probatio:

Mithridates said that his only concern through it all was to help Chaereas and he could prove his innocence by producing the perfect proof: a living Chaereas.

Conclusio:

Rather than summing up his case, Mithridates asked Chaereas to step forward.

Pandemonium broke loose as did all the pent-up emotions of both sides including those of Chaereas and Callirhoe. It is the outpouring of emotions of all kinds which Chariton claimed to be the makings of a great drama:

Who could describe such a courtroom? Did any dramatist ever produce such a scene on any stage? An observer in the courtroom would have thought that he was in a theatre filled with emotions on every side: tears, happiness, amazement, sorrow, disbelief, prayer.

After Dionysius and Chaereas had almost come to blows, Artaxerxes dismissed the various parties, acquitted Mithridates, but announced that Dionysius and Chaereas would have to plead anew their case with regard to Callirhoe before him. Artaxerxes could not bear to see Callirhoe depart and entrusted her to his queen Statira, in whose keeping Callirhoe was given a chance to relax and was protected from the curious and the sight-seers. But there was one eager sight-seer in the audience whom Statira could not keep out, the king, who was now in love with Callirhoe.

After the tiring vicissitudes of his love affair with Callirhoe, Chaereas was at his wit's ends. This last turn of events had pushed his emotions to the breaking point. He turned on Aphrodite and almost cursed her, for it was she who had given Callirhoe to him, only to take her away. Then he added a curious comment about the nature of deities: "I built you a temple, and in it I made sacrifices to you. How could you then take Callirhoe from me?"

Chariton obviously had developed a *do ut des* (I give that you might give) relationship between his characters and their gods. The mortal gives something to the deity so that the deity will give something in return. This was not only a bold anachronism of the later forms of religious worship which do not belong in the fifth-century B.C. Greek world, but it gave some insight into Chariton's conception of the relationship between mortals and their gods. Fortune or Fate, while acting many times with no regard for mortals and sometimes treating mortals as toys for entertainment, could be influenced by the actions of pious people.

This book concludes with a short speech by Dionysius and then one by Chaereas, the two principals in the upcoming trial. It is a clever yet artistic way to jump off into the next book. The mood of tension was somewhat spoiled by yet another suicide attempt of Chaereas. Chariton's delineation of the King Artaxerxes was almost absolutely conditioned by his personal conception of the oriental despot, and he was almost certainly mistaken. Artaxerxes was an oriental despot who had no need to scheme to get Callirhoe; he would have simply taken her. Chariton pictured for us a rather kindly, middle-class, nonregal despot. In this book Chariton also offered us an interesting look at his view of justice in the ancient world. Neither the just nor the unjust

(nor all the shades in between) get justice of any kind. Like
Fate, Justice *plays* with her helpless mortals.

IV   Act III (*Book 6*): *Artaxerxes in Love*

The arguments as to who should get Callirhoe were on everyone's lips: she belonged to Chaereas, though he caused her death
and buried her; she belonged to Dionysius because he rescued
her, even if he did buy her as a slave. Some of the women even
gave advice to Callirhoe whom she should marry. Since she was
married to both men, it goes without saying that she herself
was in a perfect position to judge her two husbands—to compare
notes on them, as it were. Statira, on the other hand, would be
happy to see Callirhoe go anywhere away from Artaxerxes who
has been paying far too much attention to the Greek girl. Artaxerxes, afraid he would lose Callirhoe and never see her again,
wrestled with himself about the proper course of action. Chariton
continued to portray Artaxerxes, not as an oriental despot but as
a middle-class property owner who was mired in petty details,
observant of the feelings of everyone else except his own, igno-
rant of his own strength, unaccustomed to power, and timid.
None of this reflects historical despots or despots in earlier
literature. When King David desired Bathsheba, nothing was
allowed to stand in his way; when Oedipus wanted Jocasta,
his mother, as his wife, nothing, including legal and natural
prohibitions, deterred him. Chariton's Artaxerxes was not made
of that kind of fibre. In fact, it is not at all clear that Artaxerxes
was at all times in command of the situation and cognizant of
the ramifications of his own actions. The fault for this lies clearly
with Chariton's delineation of his character.

Chariton developed an interesting love triangle of three men
(Chaereas, Dionysius, Artaxerxes) with Callirhoe in the middle.
As Chariton developed the action or plot he invariably paused
at each main character (here there are four) and described the
movements of each one, including each one's reactions to the
main thrust of the plot, before he moved on to a new development or phase of the plot. Thus, at this time we see (1) Artaxerxes summoning Artaxates, his eunuch slave, and ordering him
to postpone the trial thirty days so that he did not have to part

with Callirhoe; (2) Dionysius cursing himself for bringing Callirhoe to Babylon; (3) Chaereas trying to commit suicide by starving himself; and (4) both Callirhoe and Statira worried by Artaxerxes's growing affection for the former.

After all the loose ends were tied up, Chariton proceeded. Artaxerxes began to worship at the altar of Aphrodite, and once he had acknowledged her supremacy over all the other gods, he found himself moved to plot with Artaxates to obtain Callirhoe for his own. For a time he considered whether or not Callirhoe might be a goddess come to earth to visit torments on him. The tone of the king's words and actions was one of pain caused by unrequited love. Chariton painted here a curious picture of the king: he was more like a pining poet than a despot: Artaxates suggested he seize the girl, but the king was seriously offended:

"Never suggest such a thing again! The very thought of seducing another man's wife is abhorrent to me. I know the laws of the land which I passed and which are applicable to me as well as to my subjects. I still have my dignity."

At the suggestion of Artaxates that the king try to take his mind off Callirhoe by busying himself with other activities such as hunting, Artaxerxes staged an enormous royal hunt. It is obvious from this that Chariton had been reading Ovid's *Remedia Amoris* (*Remedies of Love*), in which Ovid advises distraught lovers to occupy themselves with many different entertainments (including hunting) until they are free of Love's terrible bonds. But the distraction failed, and Artaxates rationalized for the benefit of the king in good Sophistic fashion that the king had no real problem since Callirhoe was at that moment married to no one, but was in fact a widow. The king was pleased and agreed to follow Artaxerxes's lead, if (1) nothing was done against Callirhoe's will and (2) everything was done secretly. Artaxates saw a rosy future for himself at the king's court but, says Chariton, there was one serious problem:

Because Artaxates is a slave and eunuch, but especially because he is a barbarian, he thinks it is a simple matter to persuade Callirhoe. He has, in addition, no comprehension of Greek pride.

With the word "barbarian" Chariton implies not only the usual definition, (i.e., someone who does not speak Greek), but he means also someone who does not act in accordance with good Greek ethics. Artaxates was obviously a lesser being. Chariton's not infrequent slurs against Persians betrayed his obvious pro-Greek, anti-Persian bias. Though he lived in Aphrodisias, a part of the old Persian empire, he unequivocally aligned himself with the more recent Greek conquerors.

At the proper moment Artaxates proposed his scheme to Callirhoe, adding that when she had married the king and had many jewels and gold, she should not forget him, Artaxates, her real benefactor.

Artaxates includes himself in any future benefits to be derived from the union of Callirhoe and the king. Every slave who speaks on behalf of his master always recommends himself in addition, seeking his own advancement at every turn.

Chariton has clearly borrowed here the popular literary conception of the slave from New Comedy. In this genre the slave acts on behalf of the master only when his own case will be advanced. Artaxates also plays the role of the go-between the king and Callirhoe, a popular part for slaves in comedy (see Plautus). Chariton has simply transferred this role of the slave in comedy to the more serious scenes of ideal romance. But Callirhoe told the eunuch that she was not worthy of the great king and ran away. When she found herself alone, she repeated to herself (and thus to her reader) all the misfortunes that had befallen her. It is yet another summary of the story, a summary which betrayed Chariton's desire to keep in touch with certain conventions of oral epic. When Callirhoe mentioned suicide, Artaxates realized how untenable was his situation: since he had not won over Callirhoe, the king would be furious; the queen would hate him; Callirhoe had refused him; Chaereas and Dionysius would plot against him.

With the king becoming ever more insistent that he press Callirhoe for an affirmative answer, Artaxates delivered an ultimatum to her: either she submit willingly to the king or he would take her by force:

"Consider well your choices," said the eunuch. "Your first husband, Chaereas, will love you and honor you even more, when he realizes that you have pleased the great king." Artaxates believed what he said because he did not understand Greek character. All barbarians, it is well known, stand before their kings in fearful awe, believing them to be incarnate gods. The fact is that Callirhoe would not have married Zeus himself, preferring Chaereas to immortality.

Zeus had of course come down from Olympus and mated with Danae (begetting Perseus), with Europa (begetting Minos), with Leda (begetting Helen of Troy), but Callirhoe would have refused even his advances. In a very natural and unobtrusive manner Chariton made use again of the graphic analogue from myth, not merely as an example but rather as a symbol.

For the first time (Bk. 6.8) outside forces and movements, which were totally unrelated to the plot, moved across the path of the action: the Egyptians had revolted and sent a spearhead of forces as far East and North as Syria. The government in Babylon was in a state of alarm but reacted positively. Up until this last turn of events Chariton had kept his narrative directly concerned with the actions of the pair of lovers Chaereas and Callirhoe. This concentration focused on the two main characters, with almost complete disregard for extraneous events and characters, was a special mark of classical literature. From the classical standpoint the novel had reached its climax in the lovers' discovery that the other was still alive. From here to the final chapter the action was concerned with attempts to reunite the pair. The denouement of the novel was set, and a relaxation of the tension, which had built up since Callirhoe's apparent death, was realized. Chariton provided us with the traditional recognition scene with which all earlier fictional works (Homer's *Odyssey,* Euripides' *Electra,* Greek New Comedy, and Roman *Fabula Palliata*) most usually concluded or disentangled themselves. After this first recognition scene the lovers were parted for the last time, and a second recognition scene was required at the beginning of Bk. 8.

Artaxerxes organized his forces at hand and, ordering the outlying armies to follow as soon as possible, marched out against the Egyptians. Dionysius took his place in the line of march; Statira was instructed to follow along with Callirhoe in the king's personal baggage train.

IV Act IV (Book 7): The War

Book 5 produced the tension of the courtroom battle; Book 6 was more peaceful and concerned itself with characters moving to stronger positions; Book 7 was once again a violent section, full of war. In this alternation we can detect an attempt by Chariton to vary the tempo of his work, first by creating a highly unstable situation marked by disorder, and then by resolving at least partially the uncertainty and modifying the mood toward the subdued.

While Artaxerxes and Dionysius were engaged in making war, Chaereas searched throughout Babylon for Callirhoe. With two rivals for Callirhoe's hand, Dionysius got free of one, Chaereas, by letting slip the rumor that the great king had given Callirhoe to him in return for his help in the war against Egypt. To save Chaereas from cutting his own throat (his suicide attempts are seemingly without number), Polycharmus suggested that they join the army of the Egyptians and embarrass the King of Persia. The Egyptian king was delighted to receive Chaereas and made him one of his military advisors—after all he was the son-in-law of Hermocrates, one of the Greeks' most famous generals. At one particular briefing session when the king proposed to retreat from the area around Tyre, because the city itself had not been taken by storm, and to pull back to the fortified city of Pelusium on the coast just east of the Egyptian Delta, Chaereas stood up and opposed any kind of retreat. He was supported by many others and finally was given a command and an army to try to capture Tyre. In the Egyptian army he found a group of Greek mercenaries and from these chose three hundred to lead against Tyre. Promising to show the Tyrians the difference between Greeks and barbarians, Chaereas was elected general of the expeditionary force against Tyre. Chaereas (the spokesman here for Chariton) stressed the dissimilarity between Greeks and barbarians: Greeks were good fighters; one Greek was worth a barbarian regiment; Greeks came from noble and warlike ancestors; in warfare Greeks sought no personal riches, only glory and an undying fame (like that of Leonidas). Indeed it was to match Leonidas's three hundred Spartans at Thermopylae that Chaereas selected only three hundred Greek mercenaries. Further, in imitation of Herodotus and Thucydides, Chariton had his general Chaereas deliver an hortatory speech to his soldiers just before the battle.

Like Agamemnon and Odysseus before Troy, Chaereas tricked the Tyrians into opening the city gates and then slew the inhabitants:

Chaereas killed the Tyrian commander, attacked the others, and "struck them down on all sides; a terrible groan arose from the field" [Homer]. Like lions attacking an unguarded herd they rushed at the enemy. . . . Defenders ran from the city but found they could not retreat because the pile of corpses at the gates prevented them.

Chariton provided us with a marvelous blend of styles from Thucydidean prose to Homeric epic and epic simile. The movement of large forces of men, sieges of cities, and the smell of battle, all look back toward the Greek literary forms of epic and history. The quote from Homer and the use of one of his epic similes beg association with the epic. Still in mourning for Callirhoe, Chaereas, like an epic hero, refuses even now to wear victor's garlands. In his book Chariton moved vast forces from place to place, destroyed some forces and painted others as victors, striving to emulate all the while the classic pages of Xenophon of Athens, Thucydides, and Herodotus.

Meanwhile, Artaxerxes was filled with panic at the loss of Tyre and determined to make an all-out effort against the Egyptians. To free himself to move more quickly, Artaxerxes made the fateful decision to settle his baggage train together with Statira and Callirhoe on the island of Aradus, which lies three miles offshore and some miles north of Sidon in Phoenicia. As chance would have it, Aradus had a temple to Aphrodite. At that same time Chaereas was given command of a large contingent of the Egyptian navy because all men considered Greeks, especially Syracusans, to be the best sailors. With Chaereas in command of the fleet, the Egyptian king attacked the Persians on land but was severely repulsed, mostly because of the valor of Dionysius, who with a picked force of cavalry, cut off the Egyptian retreat and forced the Egyptian king to kill himself. After the ominous start of the war followed by its successful conclusion, Artaxerxes was so delighted, that he awarded Callirhoe as a war prize of booty to Dionysius.

We are reminded here of the great king of all the Greeks, Agamemnon, awarding Briseis to Achilles for valor and then later demanding her return. Likewise, Callirhoe was awarded to Dionysius, but he was never given the opportunity to take possession of her because of his overweening pride in thinking himself equal to the gods. Chaereas's fleet had been victorious over all the eastern Mediterranean and had captured Aradus with all the great king's baggage, his wife, and Callirhoe. Statira was extremely sad, for she believed that the whole Persian cause, including her husband, was lost. Callirhoe, captured now so many times, was beyond despair and begged for a sword to kill herself. Her Egyptian guard was "unable to console her or lend any assistance because he kept his distance from her. Barbarians have a kind of innate servility when confronted with royalty—especially of the Greek variety." The Egyptian guard reported the events surrounding Callirhoe's behavior to Chaereas, who wondered at such noble actions.

V   Act V (Book 8): All's Well That Ends Well

The last book of this novel and the last act of this play opened with a short summary of the preceding action directed by Chariton to the reader. With a fairly heavy hand Chariton explained some of the refinements woven into the fabric of the novel's structure. His love for the ironic continues: Chaereas and Callirhoe were reunited, but because of jealous Fortune neither knew the other's whereabouts:

But Aphrodite has softened her opposition to Chaereas's former pride and unreasoned jealousy of Callirhoe. Chaereas's pride stirred the *phthonos* of the gods; his jealousy of Callirhoe aroused their anger. . . .By his countless sufferings and wanderings, however, he has now redeemed himself and reconciled himself to Aphrodite.

All's well that ends well:

I am confident that all my readers will be delighted with the final book of my novel. It will stand in stark contrast to the dramatic tension and tragedies of the earlier parts. Gone are pirates, slavery, courtrooms, battles, suicides. Here to stay are love and marriage.

As Chaereas was about to board ship and leave Aradus, deserting Callirhoe "as a kind of sleeping Ariadne," his attention was directed toward the unidentified and noble slave girl. Immediately they recognized each other and just as immediately fainted. The good news was spread around at once, and crowds assembled around the couple, congratulating them. The reactions of the crowd were mirrors of the couple, and reflected their feelings. The crowd served also the function of the chorus from drama, and it relayed to the reader the general sentiments of the hero, heroine, and author. Chaereas delegated (to Polycharmus) his affairs of Ares (war) and devoted himself exclusively to the affairs of Aphrodite (love). Our hero thus reverted to form and became once again the new style hero of romance. The older type of hero of warfare like Achilles had no longer a permanent role in romantic epics like this. The work concluded, as it had begun, with a honeymoon experience. In the middle of telling their tales of woe to each other, an Egyptian officer interrupted to tell them that the Egyptian king was dead and King Artaxerxes with his army was pressing toward Aradus to rescue Statira. Chaereas, with his whole force, retreated to Paphos on Cyprus, where it was decided that all who wished it could accompany Chaereas back to Syracuse.

Before they set out for Syracuse, Callirhoe pleaded for Statira's release and transportation back to Artaxerxes. She informed Chaereas that it was Statira who had befriended her while a captive in Babylon. Needless to say, Statira was ecstatic and thankful when she learned of her release. Chariton had manipulated in this scene a very nice reversal of positions (a clear instance of Aristotle's dramatic *peripeteia*): the noble Callirhoe was now mistress over Statira; earlier in Babylon Statira had been mistress and Callirhoe the slave. Chariton made it perfectly clear to us that the Fates or Fortune, or whoever rules the universe, was fickle and not *above* humiliating the powerful or *below* exalting the lowly. To make the return trip to Artaxerxes, Chaereas appointed one Demetrius, an acquaintance of the great king, as commander of the returning ships, and in typical Charitonian overstatement and oversimplification characteristic of Greek romantic emotionalism, said "that no one went away without gaining his request from Chaereas."

Along with Demetrius he sent a letter for Artaxerxes explaining his actions in fighting with the Egyptians, his capture of Aradus, and now his return of Statira to Babylon. Callirhoe also had second thoughts about her earlier actions and felt now a certain responsibility toward Dionysius whom she had abhorred previously. In a letter, entrusted to Statira, secretly and without the knowledge of Chaereas, Callirhoe thanked Dionysius for rescuing her from pirates; she placed her son in his keeping to be raised by him, married to his daughter (by a previous marriage), and returned to Syracuse, when he had grown, to meet his grandfather, Hermocrates. She thus hid from Dionysius forever the fact that the boy was not his and from Chaereas the full circumstances surrounding the boy's birth and education in Babylon.

In an emotion-filled arrival, to which only a writer like Chariton can do justice, Artaxerxes welcomed home his wife, and Dionysius stoically bore his loss of Callirhoe. With his wife still in his embrace, Artaxerxes asked about Callirhoe, but, after reading Chaereas's letter, relayed to him by Demetrius, he understood that he also had lost her forever (to a Greek!): and said: "Chaereas must be a happy man. He is surely luckier than I am."

For the second time Chaereas had successfully beaten back a set of suitors for Callirhoe's hand. It is more important for the nature of the hero in Chariton that he be a good lover, able to ward off suitors for his wife, than that he be a great warrior on the battlefield. As a composite figure of epic creatures such as Odysseus, Chaereas is a rather pale shadow. Such a comparison is necessary, if a bit unfair. Chariton was obviously comparing Cheareas with epic heroes of the past, and in the concluding scene of the novel where Chaereas reported (like a hero-rhapsode) all his exploits to the crowd assembled in the theatre at Syracuse, he was begging us to observe the new romantic hero of the age. With all the loose ends of the story tied up in Babylon, Chariton turned his attention to Syracuse where the armada of Chaereas was sailing into the harbor. One by one Chariton described the reunions of Chaereas and Callirhoe with their parents, and luxuriated in the emotions of the moment.

The homecoming of the pair of Syracusan lovers was interesting in that Chariton pictured it as the triumphant entry of a *Roman* general into Rome. The assembled crowds, i.e., the common people, milled about Chaereas and Callirhoe, asked questions, asked how they could help, acted solicitously about the pair's health, and as much as possible involved themselves in the actions and lives of their heroes. In a vicarious fashion they lived and relived the adventures and triumphant return. The crowds acted again like the chorus in a Greek drama and set the mood of rejoicing and jubilation at the safe return of the city's most famous residents.

Chariton, of course, was vitally interested in involving the common people in the action, as much as possible, for this same type of common people were his audience and readers. Chariton's station in life placed him much more with the common people than it did with Chaereas. The crowd rushed off to the theatre (where else to hear a *drama*), and pleaded with Chaereas to fetch Callirhoe and to tell the story of his adventures beginning after the death of Theron. They knew all that transpired before his crucifixion. Then they cheered with Chaereas's successes, they groaned and wept with his misadventures, and they gasped over his tales of war in Egypt and riches in Babylon. So Chariton's common people lived vicariously in the actions of Chaereas. With the crowd listening to Chaereas in the theatre, Callirhoe stepped out of the spotlight, and Chariton followed her to the temple of Aphrodite where she prayed to her protectress and benefactor. The story concluded as Callirhoe made her thank offerings to Aphrodite. The author from Aphrodisias has thus done justice to the fame of the eponymous heroine of his city. It is not with insubstantial evidence that we suggest that Chariton's novel itself is an aretology and thank offering to Aphrodite for having made Aphrodisias a prosperous and lovely city, beautiful enough even for her presence.

CHAPTER 6

A New Kind of Hero

I Introduction

FOR much of the Western World it would not be an exaggeration to say that the ancient Greek hero represented the high point of heroism, the quintessence: Achilles the man of war, Odysseus the man of skill, and Oedipus the man of courage. The hero lived (obviously) in the heroic age, a time before, and set apart from, the Golden Age (fifth century B.C.) of Greece. The age of heroes was that time between 1500 and 800 B.C. (Homer fl. 800 B.C.) when the aristocracy in a feudal state ruled Greece in a shame culture divorced from guilt. Homer and the tragedians gave concrete form to the mythical hero, and though trapped in a guilt culture where law and order prevailed, they spoke of an earlier day where *arete*, honor, and self-mastery set heroes aside from simpler mortals.

C. H. Whitman[1] has written eloquently of the Greek hero and observes that there are two qualities which make him different from other heroes: a self-destructive nature and an intimacy with the gods. The self-destructive quality of the Greek hero is best seen in Achilles and Ajax who prefer, and in fact choose, fame and greatness before a long life. There is no Fortune or Fate which drives either hero to death. Rather it is the hero's conception of his own sense of honor, his uncompromising judgment of his role in the world, and his unflinching defense of his reputation, which kill him. To some in society he is insane; but he lives in an inner world in which he makes his own rules. He has no time for real reflection and does not rationalize his actions or make excuses for his deeds. A hero protects his reputation exclusively (shame culture) and has no concern for the social structure of right and wrong
130

(guilt culture). Heroes are closest to deities when they act like them, doing superhuman deeds and bringing boons to their fellowmen. By their actions and good works heroes aid lesser mortals and set themselves between gods and men, becoming demigods as it were. It is an interesting matter on which to speculate, whether heroes are great men, mediators between heaven and earth, disguises under which gods come to earth and act like men, or whether they reflect in the extreme (superego) the divinity that is in all men.

Much of that which makes up an early Greek hero is not the character of the hero but rather the actions of the hero, the superman of action. Furthermore, it is interesting to observe that while the actions of a hero are usually of a violent nature, they elicit no rationalization or explanation on the part of the hero. He answers only to that divinity (here equal to his understanding of his own heroic nature) within his being. Though he stands apart from this primitive society, he is a necessary and integral part of it, and his aristocratic society cannot function without him. And while he is a boon to his whole society and dispenses boons to members of his clan, he cannot moderate in any way the tension between his character as a hero and that of simple mortal men. Some smaller heroes adopt a stance of pride (*hybris*) which is punished (*ate*) by the gods, resulting in a kind of learned lesson for the hero. The real and pure hero, however, learns no lesson, identifies with the tragic men of history, and destroys himself rather than awaiting, or offering himself for, destruction. For the Greek hero the gods who built him and those who could destroy him reside within his own person and personality. He yields and changes for no one and carries out his deeds on inner direction, not like a madman who knows no law but like a demigod who acts according to inner law. Though we are far away from Greek heroes, we nevertheless seem to have a kind of understanding and real feeling for them because they are supernatural, superpolitical, and super-human.

To ancients who knew such to be heroes, Chaereas must have come as quite a shock or at least a letdown. With respect to the two qualities peculiar to early Greek heroes identified by Whitman, Chaereas exhibits both but on far different levels. He very early shows a proclivity to self-destructiveness, and threatens suicide at every turn until Books 7 and 8, where he appears more like an early ancient hero. But the attempted suicides are nothing like the undercurrent of self-destructiveness running through Ajax's character, for example. When any situation becomes too difficult and the tension too great, Chaereas tries to kill himself. Ajax, on the other hand, shapes events to fit his personal outlook and does not kill himself until after he has embarrassed and tarnished his personal reputation, and there is no longer any opportunity or hope to continue his rule as a hero. It is the active force of Ajax which dooms him; for Chaereas it is his passive role. The second way in which Chaereas is similar (yet dissimilar) to ancient heroes is his intimacy with the gods. Ajax had his deity within his character and heroic nature, while Chaereas is the plaything of Fortune, pushed around in whatever way jealous and spiteful gods wish. The deity of Jealousy is at first angry with Chaereas and only later after she relents and is appeased, does Chaereas assume a more dominant role in the action. The distinguishing mark of his relationship with the gods is his lack of aggressiveness. The divine is no longer in the hero (Ajax's case) but rather is another outside force.

Now that we have looked at the early Greek heroes and how they differ from Chariton's hero, we should examine more positively the new style, i.e., just what kind of hero Chaereas is. To begin we can say that Chaereas is a hero only in that he is the protagonist of the story; he is hardly heroic. He is very young—bordering on the immature—and in difficult and dangerous circumstances refuses to meet his challenges head-on until Book 7. In many situations, as for example Callirhoe's suitors in Book 1, he takes no active role in driving them out, nor does he take vengeance on them for incriminating and "framing" Callirhoe to make her look guilty of conspiring with other lovers. Only Hermocrates considers punishing the suitors. Chaereas does, however, confront Callirhoe with the evidence and takes action against her. In his relationship with her he is somewhat aggressive, especially after his marriage. Early Greek heroes seized what they wanted and gave no thought to the consequences of their deeds. Chaereas also does not consider the effect of his actions and in many instances acts with the abandon of an early hero. Once he has learned that Callirhoe is in Miletus, he rushes headlong in winter to retrieve her and is imprisoned for his thoughtless behavior. It is clear that he assumes a fairly active role in his personal dealings with Callirhoe but is extremely handicapped in relationships with strangers, particularly men in power. If he has any special relationship with the gods, Chariton does not point it out.

On the other hand Callirhoe, our heroine, seems to get peculiar benefits from the gods; her prayers appear to be efficacious immediately and frequently. Whatever benefits come to Chaereas and Callirhoe are just that, benefits from the gods. Ajax performs godlike deeds because of the divinity in him, and answers to no higher authority than his own heroic integrity. The impression left by Chariton in his novel is that both hero and heroine are only heroic to each other. Callirhoe's beauty is godlike, all powerful, and superhuman, and in these ways, heroic. The same can be said for Chaereas. But these are pale images and shallow reflections of full-bodied creatures like Ajax.

Chaereas and Callirhoe go through the action in the novel as characters strangely out of place (if not out of time). The powerful men, at whose mercy our hero and heroine live, rule with a less than despotic power: Hermocrates, Theron, Dionysius, Mithridates, and Artaxerxes. Rather than say that Chariton's protagonists do not measure up to the quality of earlier heroes, we would like to suggest that Chaereas (and Callirhoe) represents a new kind of hero, a romantic aristocrat. His sole concern is for Callirhoe, and he will live or die, whichever is appropriate at that particular instant, for her. For many social and political reasons the idealistic hero no longer turns outward toward society and the world, but inward to his private thoughts and emotions and to the reactions and love-in-return from his heroine. These characters of Chariton are not vying with the gods for a place in saga and legend, but are dedicated devotees of the goddess of love, Aphrodite.

The new hero also has new virtues: kindness, faithfulness (hardly an early heroic virtue), gentleness, love of peace,

abhorrence of violence (e.g., Chaereas's desire to spare Theron),
and an almost unwavering belief in the gods—especially Aphrodite. If Chariton's hero must have an earlier precedent, let it
be Paris, another follower of Aphrodite, who thought only of
Helen, though he and his whole city became embroiled in
war. And if Chaereas must have later successors or imitators,
let them be the hopeless lovers of courtly romance.

It is, in fact, in some of the medieval romances that we
find our closest analogy to Chariton's romance. The epic
hero lives in an heroic age and the tragic hero hearkens back
to that same past age. The hero of romance lives in a new age,
within a highly structured class system, enjoying an unprece-
dented leisure, and requiring a new kind of hero, one consistent
with the customs and refinements of this leisure class. The
most obvious change in the hero is that from tragic to
sentimental. The romantic hero and heroine recover from their
grim trials and proceed to richer experiences, free from the
thought that such evils will ever beset them again. The new
hero is psychologically much more complex, full of doubts, a
purposeless traveler through time and space, one who encounters and passes through a marvelous myriad of exotic
experiences, which are frequently larger than the hero himself.
Our new hero does not belong to one particular ethnic group,
though he apparently has many connections with definite and
special strata of society. He shares with many early heroes the
motif of the marvelous journey: "Of all fictions the marvelous
journey is the one formula that is never exhausted."[2] The focus
of Chariton's work frequently shifts from the hero to the strange
adventures which influence him, and so the story loses its
dependence on the hero, a dependence so important to epic
and tragedy.[3]

Borrowing an idea of Jean Frappier[4] from Arthurian studies,
we can suggest that Chariton along with the other ancient
Greek novelists, with the exception of Longus, has given his
work a general tripartite structure: (I) Opening adventures
leading to marriage or a promise of marriage; (II) Separation
and Trials; (III) Concluding adventures and final reunion.
The tripartite arrangement is, however, more than a convenience
or crutch; it arises from an organic motivation within the

plot. After the opening adventures in which Chaereas meets his lady fair, marries her, and has apparently arrived at the pinnacle of pleasure, joy, and fulfillment, he displays the terrible fault (we dare not say tragic flaw) of jealousy and faithlessness toward Callirhoe. She is then taken to a faraway country, and Chaereas is forced to abandon his place of happiness and retrieve her. The motivation for the entire story rests on Chaereas's rash act. His burst of anger and subsequent blow to Callirhoe show an heroic personality in need of help, of undergoing change, and of purification, before he can return to Syracuse and enjoy the pleasures of Callirhoe, to whom he was exposed before he was prepared. After innumerable trials, which conclude with his abortive crucifixion, Chaereas is judged a better man by the gods, one deserving of Callirhoe's love. His final act of correction is his assuming the warlike character of the ancient hero and returning Callirhoe to Syracuse. Chaereas now deserves Callirhoe and his famous father-in-law; his adventures and trials have made him a worthy hero, to be admired by his parents, loved by his wife, and worshiped by the common people of Syracuse, desperately in need of a hero.[5]

While such an interpretation is speculative, it does help to explain and give a pattern to what otherwise would be a mindless and disoriented array of adventures. Rather than following Chaereas on a circuitous journey, we find our hero pursuing a fairly direct approach to expiate his guilt.

The plot structure of *The Adventures of Chaereas and Callirhoe* does not proceed directly from problem to solution. The story opens with the erotic problem of Chaereas's mad desire for Callirhoe and vice versa. This problem, however, is resolved with dispatch and the pair are quickly married. After the opening scenes of tension, a release is found in marriage and a life together. We see here a structure with one movement. But immediately everything is turned upside down, and the one-movement structure (problem-resolution) finds itself attached to a second. Book 1 contains the preliminary materials, and is followed by a book of transitional filling. The action of the hero begins again in Book 3, when Chaereas, realizing that his old world has fallen apart because of a personal mistake, sets out on a quest for Callirhoe. He begins this quest for many reasons: love for Callirhoe; desire to prove himself to Hermocrates and Syracuse; and a need to expiate his sin against Callirhoe. The first section of the story reveals a terrible fault in Chaereas's makeup; the second section is the quest. Chaereas embarks on his quest, a timeworn motif from many literatures, because he cannot function in his old environment until he is a more stable figure convinced of and believing in his own personal identity, freed of past errors, and convinced for certain of his own strength. Such a hero as Chaereas has been dealt with by Joseph Campbell, who sees in the quest myth the "monomyth" of all literature:

The mythological hero, setting forth from his . . . castle, is . . . carried away, or else voluntarily proceeds, to the threshold of adventure. There he encounters a shadow presence that guards the passage. . . . Beyond the threshold, then, the hero journeys through a world of unfamiliar yet strangely intimate forces, some of which severely threaten him (tests), some of which give magical aid (helpers). When he arrives at the nadir of the mythological round, he undergoes a supreme ordeal and gains his reward. The triumph may be represented as the hero's sexual union with the goddess-mother of the world . . . , his recognition by the father-creator. . . . If the powers have blessed the hero, he now sets forth under their protection . . . , if not, he flees and is pursued. . . . The boon that he brings restores the world (elixir).[6]

While Chaereas is hardly as sophisticated or complex as Campbell's description of the mythical hero, we seriously doubt that any single hero fulfills these requirements. Obviously, the hero himself is not aware of the archetypal structure of his being, nature, or quest. But Chaereas does in the main fit Campbell's heroic mold. At the beginning of Chariton's work, we can perceive that Hermocrates is the strongest male influence among the main characters and among the close relatives of either Chaereas or Callirhoe. His influence, however, is directed by force and military prestige. After Chaereas has departed from Syracuse, recognizing his unjust acts, he enters the strange and marvelous adventureland of the *East*. There he undergoes a series of tests or ordeals. To many of them he is unequal, but with the aid of outside forces, like Mithridates and certain favorable deities, he proves himself equal to the task of fetching Callirhoe; he wins his spurs by defeating the Persians. Back in Syracuse he appears on an equal footing with Hermocrates as a hero. At the approach of Chaereas's fleet in the harbor of Syracuse, the people inform Hermocrates of a possible attack. In this scene we see Chaereas confronting the old hero of Syracuse and then, without pushing him aside, surpass him in the eyes of all the people.

Chaereas is a new kind of hero, who fights only if he must, but who takes his place as a hero through gentleness, devotion to his mistress, social graces, and conformity to the ideals of a leisure class. The old hero of Greek epic no longer finds a home in the minds of the Greek people of Chariton's class. Such a hero is too wild, unpredictable, and governed by laws which he himself has made. The stratified society, to which Chariton speaks and of which he himself is a member, is established on written laws, which tend to equalize the great and small, and on unwritten laws of society which, like good manners, allow all people to live together in a kind of peace. An ancient hero in such a society as this would be like a bull in a china shop.

The progress of the young lover Chaereas into the mature lover and sometimes brave warrior might be called the *rites de passage,* a term made popular by anthropologists to indicate the initiation rites of a young person in a primitive society from childhood into manhood. Each youth in such a primitive society is usually cast out of his clan into the wilderness to prove himself a man and to return to make positive contributions to his people. While Chaereas surely does not live in what anyone would call a primitive society, Chariton (and many other writers) has seemingly borrowed or merely fashioned his hero according to the *rites de passage,* which he inherited from his ancestors. The *rites de passage* are a common inheritance of all people, and a symbol of growth of any young man, who is also a hero. The maturation of a young man into a hero, a type of "the marvelous journey . . . the one formula that is never exhausted," is a literary interpretation of the *rites de passage.* It seems that the *rites de passage* mean also a journey into the

unknown and afterward a return home. The journey comprises
(1) separation, (2) isolation, (3) death of the old, and (4)
symbolic rebirth. This pattern of the *rites de passage,* with its
symbols now set out in detail by Eliade and Campbell, was
apparently not known to Chariton, who obviously recognized
the journey motif, the transformation of Chaereas, and his
growth into a kind of hero, but whose understanding fell far
short of comprehending the underlying monomyth. Modern
social anthropology with its comparative methodology, mythology as a science, and archetypal investigations of literature
and life, have gone beyond Chariton's simple story of human
existence as a passage of man through time.

The last part of the journey (the monomyth), the last hurdle
in the *rites de passage* after the wanderer has undergone his
ordeals and is reborn a hero, is in many ways the most
interesting:

> The full round . . . of the monomyth, requires that the hero . . . begin
> the labor of bringing . . . the Golden Fleece, or his sleeping princess,
> back into the kingdom of humanity, where the boon may rebound to
> the renewing of the community.[7]

The wandering Chaereas, having returned home, is now surely a
kind of hero. He has gone through trials and ordeals, come close
to death, defeated the enemy on the field of battle, and rescued
a fair lady in distress. He has many of the attributes of a hero
and some of his deeds were heroic. Home again in Syracuse he
is acknowledged by relatives and citizens to be a hero. But what
is the boon that Chaereas brings back with him, or which accompanies him and which sets him above, and apart from, other
men? Simply put, the boon is the power of love, in this case
the love of Chaereas for Callirhoe. In the beginning of the story
Chaereas fails to use the power of love; he is jealous and un-
trusting of Callirhoe, and is consequently (because of Callirhoe's
apparent death at Chaereas's hands) forced to undergo trials
and ordeals until Aphrodite, the goddess of love or Love per-
sonified, releases him from the wheel of torture. The love of
Callirhoe for Chaereas did not change him in the beginning; he
remained suspicious and egocentric. After the ordeals and the

trip to Babylon, he recognizes for the first time what he had lost when Callirhoe died, and the sight of her alive and the chance to win her back spur him on to conquer Artaxerxes, her captor. Chaereas is redeemed by love. He forgives Artaxerxes, has no further malice toward Dionysius, and sends Statira, his captive, back to her husband. He returns home to the delight of his parents and brings back Callirhoe, a kind of boon, who delights her parents, the assembled people, and her husband. The love of Callirhoe for Chaereas is a power which in our story alters the pages of history, saves two powerful families from destruction and despair, and rebounds to the credit and eternal glory of Aphrodite, the personification of the power of love.[8]

We believe that while the seemingly endless assortment of events, ordeals, and narrow escapes of hero and heroine do present an apparent lack of design and structure, underneath the somewhat disjointed outward form lies a very real inner unity: through ordeal and hardship an individual can be tempered into a stronger man and with the love of a virtuous woman become a recognized hero. Not only do we see a design in the inner unity of the story, but also in the structure of the *matière*. With the aid of two charts we would like to show that Chariton placed, without a doubt, an external structure on his novel. In the first chart we attempt to show a *Pattern of Symmetry*: the even numbered books are sections of peace and relative calm, while the odd numbered ones are full of action and suspense. Thus every other book relieves the tension which the previous one had built up. A more important pattern for the whole work is that of axial symmetry in the arrangement of individual books.

Book 1 matches Book 8: in the first book Chaereas finds Callirhoe in a procession to the temple of Aphrodite, but she is taken away from Syracuse; in the eighth book Chaereas is reunited with Callirhoe by the direct intervention of Aphrodite and takes her back to Syracuse. In Book 2 Dionysius obtains Callirhoe under suspicious circumstances and is hopeful of getting her for a wife; in Book 7 Dionysius deceives Chaereas into thinking that Artaxerxes has given Callirhoe to him, a lie which later in this book becomes reality when Artaxerxes rewards Dionysius with Callirhoe for valor in battle. Book 3 matches 6: in Book 3 Chaereas becomes a slave of Mithridates, and in Book 6 he is freed from enslavement. Books 4 and 5 make up the axis or core of our symmetrical story: in Book 4 Chaereas reaches the lowest point in his ordeals when he mounts the cross in preparation for execution. He is saved, however, by Mithridates who encourages him to write a letter to Callirhoe which precipitates the trial and action in Book 5. The same Mithridates who saved him in Book 4, forces him to go to

PATTERN OF SYMMETRY

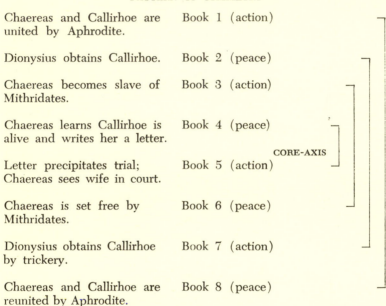

Chaereas and Callirhoe are united by Aphrodite.

Book 1 (action)

Dionysius obtains Callirhoe.

Book 2 (peace)

Chaereas becomes slave of Mithridates.

Book 3 (action)

Chaereas learns Callirhoe is alive and writes her a letter.

Book 4 (peace)

CORE-AXIS

Letter precipitates trial; Chaereas sees wife in court.

Book 5 (action)

Chaereas is set free by Mithridates.

Book 6 (peace)

Dionysius obtains Callirhoe by trickery.

Book 7 (action)

Chaereas and Callirhoe are reunited by Aphrodite.

Book 8 (peace)

Babylon for trial in Book 5. As Book 4 marks the nadir of Chaereas's life, so Book 5, which tells of Chaereas's first glimpse of Callirhoe since her apparent death, marks his return to life and hope. The trial scene of Book 5 in which it is published openly that both young lovers are alive, is the dramatic climax of the whole story. With his own eyes Chaereas has seen Callirhoe alive. It is now merely a matter of bringing home his bride. The object of such structural symmetry is to focus attention on Books 4 and 5 (especially 5) by surrounding this core with matching incidents, whose arrangement points toward the high point, the climax.

In the second chart we try to show graphically another type of framework: on the left is the *Tripartite Structure* into which the work breaks down according to *sens*. Under the *Development of the Hero* we show a hero separated by steps from his familiar environment in Books 1 through 4. In Book 5 he neither moves away from the familiar or toward it. In Books 6-8 he returns from the unfamiliar to the familiar, only after he has been tested and proved by ordeal. Because he is a changed man, aware of the power of Fortune, redeemed by the will of Aphrodite, he brings back to Syracuse a boon, a living example of the power of love.

TRIPARTITE STRUCTURE	DEVELOPMENT OF THE HERO
Adventure and Marriage	Book 1. Marriage-Separation of Chaereas from his parents, then separation from his wife.
	Book 2. Chaereas loses wife (source of power) to Dionysius.
	Book 3. Chaereas is separated from homeland and then from his personal freedom.
Separation and Trials	Book 4. Chaereas is separated from everything Greek (i.e., the familiar) in Babylon.
	Book 5. Chaereas sees Callirhoe but cannot possess her physically—power of love unrejuvenated. Climax in the plot.
	Book 6. Chaereas is freed from slavery and begins journey home.
	Book 7. Chaereas obtains power from the gods and gives boon to his foreign friends.
Final Reconciliation	Book 8. Chaereas recovers Callirhoe, and gives boon to parents, friends, and all of Syracuse.

II *The Minor Characters in Chariton*

The minor characters are interesting and worthy of study because Chariton thought they were worthy of his effort. Apparently, it is and has been the pattern to expend the most energy and time on the central figures—in Greek novels these are the pairs of lovers—and to give lesser attention to secondary actors. This may be a quite natural phenomenon and its observation here a begging of the obvious. Chariton also gives a disproportionate share of attention to his hero and heroine. But if we carefully compare Chariton's work with the other four Greek novels, plus *Apollonius of Tyre* in Latin (Petronius's *Satyricon* and Apuleius's *Metamorphoses* excepted), we will surely observe that the minor characters in Chariton are better delineated and perform more valuable functions.

By the way in which we outline our discussion of the minor characters, we will probably also distort in some way their actual importance. We will try to avoid this. Natural divisions are male=female, or Greek=barbarian, or free=slave; but natural divisions are not necessarily productive, though they may be revealing. A division of male-female minor characters does not seem to yield much, except perhaps in a negative way: male and female minor characters (like our hero and heroine) do not apparently exhibit major differences. For example, Plangon and Artaxates scheme in much the same way to bring about favorable results to their masters. Greek men (and women), however, are described frequently as more noble than barbarians: Hermocrates does not waver from his principles; Artaxerxes rationalizes away all legitimate objections to his keeping Callirhoe for himself. The nobility of free women (or men) is stressed in character-revealing incidents: though Callirhoe has been brought into her house and though Artaxerxes is obviously in love with Callirhoe and almost throwing it in her teeth, Statira is above rebuking him or in any way punishing Callirhoe; Plangon, on the other hand is concerned about the welfare of her master, Dionysius, and of her charge, Callirhoe, but is not above acting to their disadvantage when she believes her personal interest might gain some advantage.

A. *Minor Characters: Freemen and Slaves*

Though very important people in their own right, Hermocrates and Ariston are minor characters in the plot of this story. As frequently happens, even in contemporary fiction, the author sets or adorns his stage with famous personages but then quickly drops them once the scene is drawn. The backdrop and atmosphere are clear to the reader or audience. The reasons why Chariton leaves Hermocrates and Ariston as thin characters are not hard to imagine: (1) from history they are well-known, while Chaereas is fictional; (2) a strong historical character will drive the fictional one from the stage; and (3) Chariton is primarily interested in fiction. It is impossible to detect from the character portrayal of Hermocrates, Callirhoe's father, or Ariston, Chaereas's father, any peculiarities, idiosyncrasies, or traits inherited by their children. In other words the two fathers are window dressing, and, vis-à-vis their children's life and actions, have no cause-effect relationships. Though Hermocrates is surely a man of action, he takes none of that action against the jealous suitors who caused Callirhoe's apparent death. Chariton remarks that Hermocrates has his eye on the former suitors, but does not follow it up with a separate episode where Hermocrates takes vengeance on them. Hermocrates does show some individuality of mind when he disagrees with Chaereas about the punishment of Theron and exerts enough personality to convince the people of Syracuse to impale Theron. He himself, however, does not conduct the search for Callirhoe. Chariton assigns the search to Chaereas; this is an important point because it moves our future hero out of the shadow of his historically important father-in-law. Chaereas's own father, Ariston, plays no role except to be identified as Chaereas's father. It is as though Chaereas and Callirhoe, being good middle-class characters, needed parents; their mothers are completely faceless except when someone is needed to cry. We are safe to hazard a guess that to a large degree the role of Hermocrates was created to serve as a model for the kind of hero Callirhoe should have as a husband. He is no foil. What Hermocrates represents to the people of Syracuse—savior of the nation—at the beginning of our novel, the reader is asked to look for the same from Chaereas at the end of the novel.

Leonas and Theron are fascinating creations. But since there is a good deal of uncertainty whether Leonas is a freeman or a slave, and since he fits better into our scheme under the rubric Greek-barbarian, we will place him there. Theron is the pirate and will become a class by himself. The husband and wife team of Phocas and Plangon is set in perspective if we compare the team with the freeborn friend of Chaereas, Polycharmus. In character development Phocas and Polycharmus are not worthy of note. Phocas is virtually a name only and Polycharmus a mere foil to Chaereas. But Polycharmus does serve a vital function; he is the strength to keep Chaereas from committing suicide, and when Chaereas refuses to save himself from crucifixion at the hands of Mithridates's soldiers, he assumes an optimistic posture and saves Chaereas. While his character development is thin, his type of character is aristocratic, and the advice he gives to Chaereas is aristocratic. He encourages him to search for Callirhoe, after she is sold as a slave; he gives him positive advice at every turn, determined by Chaereas's best interests not his own. Chariton has established altruism as a mark of the aristocratic nature. Freemen and women, who in this novel are almost synonymous with aristocratic men and women, regularly conduct themselves and their business in the best interest of others. While slaves are not at all times selfish, they are clearly more so than the freemen; and in the hierarchy of the aristocracy, the Greek nobles are less selfish than the barbarian. Such bearing of the aristocracy is displayed also in the minor characters.

Plangon is at once one of Chariton's best characters, one of the memorable slaves from ancient literature, and also a recognizable type character from New Comedy and mime. She is clearly typecast as the mischievous slave who tends to her master's (Dionysius) business, but who carefully notices how this business can be turned to her own benefit. From extant evidence it seems clear that people of all social and economic classes were aware of, and in fact expected, certain important slave roles in literature to display or illustrate this motif of the cunning slave. In addition to the prominence of this role in New

Comedy and its popularity with the set of people who attended the theatre, the cunning slave was also operative in the Aesopic or fabulistic tradition, which reached into the middle and lower classes, i.e., the audience of Chariton and Greek fiction.

Aesop, according to tradition, was one of the common people and almost surely a slave. Aesop (given here as one individual, but probably a series of persons) spoke for the practicality and usefulness of actions and deeds; he spoke for a morality that was practical and a native wit associated with those educated in the school of life and hard knocks. The Aesopic tradition grew up from the middle and lower classes and spoke to the needs of those classes and also in a way has projected the morality of these classes for us to see. The slave Aesop could have found a job as one of the slaves in Chariton's novel.

Slaves had grown up under the direction of situation ethics. Venial sins of slaves were overlooked as necessary expressions of the slave-soul. As those of middle-class morality saw themselves, the aristocrats, and the slaves, so they projected and restrained and erected literary traditions: saints are not completely virtuous and sinners are not totally without redeeming social value. The Greek *hetaerae* (prostitutes) were never morally depraved; perhaps misguided or disoriented. To these *hetaerae* were permitted excesses of all kinds—because they were slaves, and slaves were different from others. To the aristocrats another set of values was applied: their personalities and their actions were expected to be larger than life. Because aristocrats performed great deeds, certain of their actions could be overlooked: the personal lives of aristocrats never had to be on the lofty level of their state lives. To the middle classes who made up Chariton's audience, *hetaerae* were free of any sense of shame, aristocratic women were required to maintain a façade, at least, of respectability, but middle-class women demanded of their own behavior a strict adherence to conservative and traditional morality.

This middle-class Greek view of the world and its inhabitants tempered the nature of the characters of Chariton's novel. Plangon, a slave, is not permitted the excesses of other slaves portrayed in literature intended for different classes. Theron, the pirate, is not a vicious pirate; Artaxates, the eunuch slave, retains a fairly level balance of propriety; Artaxerxes, the king,

exercises power but not the oriental despotic kind. Some middle-
class influences are apparently clearly at work in the shaping of
the characters in Chariton's novel. Excesses permitted to slaves
and aristocrats in other genres are not permitted here. In a
real sense characters are expected to conform to this ideal. Once
the ideal is established, and this could have happened before
Chariton wrote his book, it is of no consequence whether or
not new writers subscribe to the middle-class morality. The
writers of novels subscribe to what has become a literary (as
opposed to a social) ideal and convention.

Plangon is a literary product of this ideal. In her literary mind
at least three forces are striving for allegiance: devotion to
Dionysius; pity for Callirhoe; and innate reactions for self-
preservation and survival, i.e., freedom from slavery. All three
are warring within her soul and create a special tension in the
plot. If she fails in her attempt to force Dionysius to grant her
and her husband their freedom, she is certain of slavery until
the day she dies and perhaps even added punishments including
the loss of her favored position. Her actions and dealings with
Callirhoe put her whole future in jeopardy. Within the overall
tension of the story and its main characters, Plangon by her
own will creates tension among the minor characters. She acts
quite apart from the advice of her husband, Phocas, and in fact
has assumed an amazingly dominant position in the family for
a Persian woman (or, for that matter, a Greek woman).

Plangon is clearly devoted to Dionysius, and just as clearly
devoted in her own fashion. Dionysius entrusts his most valued
possession, Callirhoe, to her. It is immediately apparent to
Plangon that Dionysius is in love with Callirhoe but cannot,
for some reason, or will not, take possession of her. Without
being told (for slaves are clever if nothing else), she moves to
bring Dionysius and Callirhoe together. She gains Callirhoe's
pity by telling her that unless she intercedes, Dionysius will
cruelly torture Phocas. Callirhoe's first plea for Phocas's life is
honored by Dionysius, who now becomes a creditor to Callirhoe
(who owes Dionysius something for the gift) and a debtor to
Plangon. Callirhoe's unexpected pregnant state gives Plangon
yet another opportunity to make herself invaluable, a creditor to
both Dionysius and Callirhoe. Plangon's suggestion to Callirhoe

to complete her pregnancy and fool Dionysius into believing the child is his endears her to Callirhoe, who gets to keep her first child, and to Dionysius, who gets his beloved. Later Callirhoe, who married the prince only to keep her child, gives it up to the prince, who in turn loses Callirhoe. By the end of the novel Plangon's good work is totally undone, and it remains for Dionysius a cruel hoax. For the child is not his: he has neither his wife nor the genuine offspring of their love. The child is Chaereas's and while Plangon had convinced Callirhoe to save the life of her unborn child (by working on her motherly instincts), Callirhoe had failed to notice the faults in Plangon's thinking. The child survived, but Callirhoe's faithfulness died. The only real winner in the series of intrigues is Plangon, who bought her freedom at a terrible price to those around her. In this area Chariton has written character portrayals more serious than his comic models of slaves. Gripus in Plautus's *Rudens* was just as eager as was Plangon to win freedom by acquiring a treasure which his master would accept at the price of freedom. But in the *Rudens* only the evil pimp lost in the end.

Within the scope of the above evidence, we hope to have held up the character of Plangon to something like illuminating scrutiny and to have shown that it is many-sided, quite human, a type in certain aspects, but also a warm creation which smacks more of realism and less of idealism than many characters in Greek novels.

By the acclaim of all Persians Statira, wife of king Artaxerxes, and Rhodogyne are the loveliest female creatures on earth. When Rumor comes talking of Callirhoe's beauty, the Persian women are openly scornful of the story, and plan how best to shame this upstart: "There is no doubt that Greeks are incorrigible braggards."

They arrange that Rhodogyne be a welcoming committee of one and greet Callirhoe at the gate. The object is to embarrass and humiliate Callirhoe, thus restoring the fame and preeminence of Persian beauty. As only the reader can guess, Rhodogyne is no match for the Greek beauty. Gracefully, without losing stride, Rhodogyne surrenders and joins the procession of Callirhoe. She has entered an ordeal with Callirhoe and lost in the manner of an aristocratic princess, lost to a woman of divine beauty, but not lost face. The aristocratic background and bearing of the woman stand her in good stead when the situation becomes demanding. She does not retreat, give vent to her emotions, or strike out at her foe. She exhibits all the signs of breeding that the ancients expected from aristocracy. Her continued or further struggle against Callirhoe would have proved her a baser being. Aristocrats have a deeper understanding of the ways and tricks of Fate; in fact, they understand better than the lower classes the strange and predestined actions of the gods and people, their playthings on earth. Aristocrats know the ways of the gods, so to speak, because within the great chain of being they are closer to the controlling powers of the universe than are the slaves. Slaves tend to relate everything to their own immediate needs and appetites and so frequently miss or fail to appreciate the import of all their responses to outside influences. In Rhodogyne's brief appearance in our story, she reflects well the image of the aristocrats which we have come to associate with the ancient world.

Statira is a regal individual. Emotionally, she is a product of the ancient world, which adhered to the old German dictum about the desirability of keeping women barefoot, pregnant, and behind the stove. Although the role of women in fifth-fourth centuries B.C. Persia is a completely dark area (so far as we can ascertain), it is logical to assume that Chariton patterned the social milieu of the Persian court after the structure of an aristocratic Greek family. As the ward of her father, the young aristocratic girl grows up within the confines of the family estate. She does not do for herself what others (slaves) can do for her; she has no intercourse with the outside world; her view of reality is that seen through the eyes of her father. At a very young age (fifteen or perhaps younger) she is married to a man who is well known to her father and, as is frequently the case, twenty years her senior. Confinement in her father's house is translated into confinement in her husband's house. In her new home she does not meet her husband's friends, especially his male friends. Only on very special occasions would a male relative of hers be allowed into her apartments. At a formal dinner party in her own home she would not be in attendance. The male guests would bring their *hetaerae,* and the husband might ask his *hetaera* to come. Very likely the host would provide a selection of *hetaerae* for the party; in the same way he would offer a mixture of entertainment. The laws on adultery between a nobleman and a noblewoman were strict; *hetaerae* and slaves were outside the laws of adultery, and sexual relations between married master and slave, in the eyes of the law and male society, were not thought of as adulterous. The ancient social structure conspired at every turn to keep society segregated and male oriented.

In such a society it is easy to understand the passive nature of aristocratic women. Rhodogyne has poise but no experience. Statira falls into the same class, and by comparison with Plangon leads an uneventful life. She is the passive subject, Plangon the active. Imprisoned in her own palace, Statira does not have the freedom of mobility offered to slaves. Statira is in her apartment (where else!) when word comes that a juicy trial is about to take place involving the prettiest girl in the world; every male seemingly wants the same girl. The aristocratic women, unable to control the movement of events in any way because of their isolation, but determined at least to make a symbolic gesture to the foreign invasion, send out Rhodogyne to meet the challenge. Lacking in beauty, compared to Callirhoe, Rhodogyne is in no way equipped to deal with the circumstances once she realizes that she is something less than Callirhoe. Statira herself takes no role in this minor female rebellion; in fact we are not given even a hint of her reactions to it. Artaxerxes, Statira's husband, places Callirhoe in her keeping until the trial is over because he himself has fallen in love with her and wants her close at hand. Statira, however, is quick to observe that his visits have now become more frequent and that he is more attentive. But Callirhoe is no concubine; she is herself a kind of royalty and capable of replacing Statira in the queenship.

The love triangle is now highly unstable, and some rash act or other could easily destroy the tranquillity, when it is announced that the Egyptians have invaded Persia. Artaxerxes prepares for war and orders that Statira and Callirhoe accompany the Persian army on their journeys in the war. Such an order is highly irregular, since wives remained at home to watch over the kingdom or the estate. Soldiers of all ranks took their mis-

tresses on expeditions but never their wives. In this particular
campaign Artaxerxes is forced to take along Statira because
he knows she must take along Callirhoe. Statira is surely aware
of her unusual attendance in her husband's camp. Fate has
another trick up her sleeve, and in the changing fortunes Chaereas captures Callirhoe and Statira as war booty. Statira is
crushed, not only for herself, but for Artaxerxes who she believes
must also have been caught. Her small world, dependent totally
on her husband, is finished. Fortune changes again quickly, and
she is returned home. Her reactions to this are predictable.

A strange thing has happened in the meantime between
Callirhoe and Statira; they have become the best of friends,
commiserating on their deteriorating situations. As the story
evolves, it is clear that Statira and Callirhoe, as women, have
more things in common and more causes to unite them than
they have suspicions to drive them apart. Though from opposite
sides of the world, so to speak, they have shared a relatively
common background and react in similar fashion to their treatment as objects. Clearly, Callirhoe has confided to Statira that
she would kill herself before giving in to the king. The friend-
ship that springs up between the two women has the practical
result of freeing Statira and returning her to Babylon. In this
instance a minor character closely resembles a major one
because they share basic ties: a common sex, similarly segregated backgrounds, and isolation from loved ones. The world
and life of Statira are in many aspects a microcosm of Callirhoe's
world with its tales of horror. Both are born free, but, because
both are female, both become slaves.

The last individual we would like to examine under the rubric,
"Freeman and Slaves" is Artaxates, eunuch slave to Artaxerxes,
king of Persia. As we have pointed out elsewhere, Artaxerxes
does not represent the eastern despot whom we learn about from
history. He is a much milder man, almost an enlightened mon-
arch, one who is interested in the personal freedom of his subjects. We see here the image of a Persian ruler as reconstructed
by a Greek looking through rosy Greek glasses. His chief eunuch,
however, is a totally different man. We might imagine him as
the alter ego of Artaxerxes. Where Artaxerxes appeals to law, he
appeals to force to get his way; where Artaxerxes moves toward

moderation, he rushes to extremes; where Artaxerxes searches his soul to learn his true feelings, he rationalizes his feelings to fit his appetites. In short, Artaxates would have made a first-rate oriental despot.

We first come upon Artaxates after the king has sent Callirhoe into his wife's apartments. The king is already in love with Callirhoe and in a roundabout fashion tells this to Artaxates, who immediately sets in motion a plan to persuade her to reject both Chaereas and Dionysius in favor of the king. We do not know that Artaxates thought that, by persuading the girl to marry Artaxerxes, he would gain freedom for himself. Rather he seems to act out of fear of the king. Artaxates begins calmly and in a pleading fashion with Callirhoe, who turns down his suggestion, and then he switches to veiled threats. Callirhoe had been subjected to pressures somewhat like this before when Plangon convinced her to marry Dionysius. But Plangon encouraged Callirhoe; she did not threaten her. It appears to us that this episode in Babylon with Artaxates and Callirhoe is a doublet or twin to that earlier episode with Plangon, and that Chariton has not created a new scene but has only altered the first one slightly. Callirhoe is thus not going through a new ordeal, merely a repetition of an old one.

In a study of the character of Artaxates it is interesting to note his inclination to violence and threats, his disrgeard for established precedents, and his proclivites to extralegal devices. The paucity of details regarding specific measures employed by Persian monarchs in the day-to-day administration of their empire precludes our making accurate judgments about the verisimilitude of Chariton's description of Artaxerxes's court. From the internal evidence alone supplied by Chariton, we can observe that Artaxates is a lawless individual and Artaxerxes a law-abiding one. In fact Artaxerxes feels obliged and constrained to follow and subject himself to his own laws. In so doing he is imitating Dionysius. Artaxates will resort to any means to achieve his end of pleasing the king. In so doing he is imitating Plangon. For this novel Chariton has "typed" slaves as basically lawless characters, and in so doing is following the literary convention of Greek New Comedy and Roman comedy.

Artaxerxes in fact becomes angry with Artaxates for even sug-

CHARITON

gesting that he seize Callirhoe by force. It appears that the king
expects his eunuch to win over Callirhoe for him, but that he
does not want to have anything to do with it or to know anything
about how it is done. If his slave resorts to underhanded methods, he can be excused because he is a slave. The king fully
expects to enjoy the pleasing end results but prefers not to be
involved in the dirty means. After Artaxates suggests that the
king merely take Callirhoe, the king is offended (6.3):

"Never at any time will I permit you to counsel me to fornicate
with another man's wife. I made the laws; I saw to it that they
were enacted; by obeying my own laws I set an example for all.
I am in complete control of myself and my emotions. Do not believe
that for one minute I would stoop to adultery."

Such stern words take Artaxates by surprise. Nevertheless, Artaxates knows that the king still desires Callirhoe and that life
around the palace would be very pleasant if he had her. With
good sophistic logic, acquired through long experience only and
not at any school, Artaxates proposes two reasons why the king
can take Callirhoe at any time that he wishes: in the first place,
she is so beautiful that she must be a goddess and therefore
the wife of no one; in the second place, Chaereas buried his
wife, thus dissolving the marriage, and Dionysius's later marriage
to her is illegal because at that time she was still married to
Chaereas. Impeccable logic! Chariton offers little or no third-
person description of his minor characters; he creates them out
of their own mouths and actions.

B. *Minor Characters: Greeks and Barbarians*

As we pointed out elsewhere, Chariton had a definite Greek
bias. In ordinary narrative he does not normally disparage things
Persian or non-Greek. But when there is a confrontation of
peoples, ideas, methods, character, or values, things Greek are
better, braver, superior. The standard Greek definition of a
barbarian is one who does not speak Greek, but utters "bar bar."
No Persian is described or portrayed as an evil or malicious individual. Chariton himself was born in the old Persian empire,
and refrains from ·ystematically criticizing his neighbors; he
does, however, admire more the Greek mind and spirit.

The number of minor Greek characters is small because so little time is spent in Greek lands. The parents of our hero and heroine qualify, as does Polycharmus; the characters at Miletus, Dionysius, Leonas, Plangon, and Phocas, are probably Greek, but this cannot be proved. Mithridates, governor of Caria, is probably Persian; his name belies a Persian origin. Pharnaces, governor of Lydia and Ionia is Persian, as are all the people in Babylon. The individuals in Egypt and the men in Chaereas's army and navy are too shadowy to constitute vital characters.

Chariton makes few statements actually about the differences between Greeks and barbarians. It is easier to see the distinctions between freemen and slaves. Economic and social class differences seem to be most important to Chariton. For instance, aristocrats are braver than the lowest classes of people; Theron's group of cutthroats contained a large number of cowards. Without necessarily referring to any one character but rather referring to all barbarians, Chariton observes the following national characteristics: (1) barbarians think of their rulers as gods and grovel before kings, whereas Greeks regard highly virtue only; (2) barbarians are hopelessly romantic, e.g., the whole population of Babylon falls in love with Callirhoe; (3) Statira notes that the Greeks are known all over the world as terrible braggarts; (4) Among the Greeks, who are generally meddlesome, the Athenians are downright busybodies, remark Theron and others; and (5) Chaereas chooses Greek soldiers for his army because (ever since Alexander's army) they make the best fighters and at will can defeat barbarians.

Primary characteristics depend on social status; nationalistic features are secondary. Chariton sums it up nicely when he says that all slaves are alike (6.5):

Every slave who talks about his master and his business to one of his own social superiors always puts in a good word for himself and seeks in every conversation of this type to gain some personal advantage.

C. *Minor Characters: Male and Female*

The material relating to this section has been taken care of largely under point A above, Freemen and Slaves. In this novel, not only the major female characters but also the minor ones are treated as slaves; in some ways aristocratic females have more constraints on them than do slaves. If the characters are female aristocrats, they are expected to be faithful, beautiful, and subservient; if female slaves, they must be aggressive, clever, and unscrupulous. Even the heroine Callirhoe is a passive character. Later on in Xenophon of Ephesus's novel and in Heliodorus's and Achilles Tatius's, we will meet up with more active females who begin to share some of the responsibility for the novel's plot and action with the male leads.

D. *Theron*

We suppose that it is always very difficult to tell who the good "guys" are and how good they are, unless we have a bad guy. Theron fills the role of bad guy. In the opening chapter of the novel Callirhoe's father, Hermocrates, almost assumes the role of a bad father when he refuses at first to approve the marriage of his daughter. Then when Chaereas kicks his wife to death (false death), he appears to be the villain. This view is altered when we see Callirhoe alive and Chaereas redeem himself. In Miletus, Dionysius, Leonas, and Plangon are seen temporarily as evil people, but in such extreme circumstances as apply in Miletus, their actions are justified. In Babylon, Callirhoe is under the protection of Statira, and Artaxerxes, though in heat, offers no immediate threat. Through it all he is a kindly, middle-aged king. Artaxates is clearly a present menace, but before he can effect any permanent evils, Fate and an Egyptian uprising intercede. Left to his own devices, however, Artaxates is not necessarily an evil man. Recognizing his king's taste in women and that kings' hints and unarticulated desires are in fact commands, Artaxates acts out of basic instincts of self-preservation.

Chaereas also meets certain (at least partially) evil individuals. The suitors for Callirhoe's hand do everything in their power to ruin the early days of Chaereas's marriage and are personally responsible for the apparent death of Callirhoe. In Miletus, Phocas tries to have Chaereas murdered by a group of wandering cutthroats, but he escapes death. Mithridates tries to use Chaereas to get to Callirhoe, but all his efforts fail. Dionysius, knowing Chaereas is alive and that he and Callirhoe are still in love and legally married, tries through many and devious ways to keep them apart. On the other hand, he did rescue Callirhoe from Theron.

An analysis of all the characters results in the conclusion that the story has only one villain, Theron. All the troubles in the whole novel spring from Theron's seizing Callirhoe in the tomb. His actions are not spur-of-the-moment type or forced upon him by present emotions. Rather, with a cold and calculating mind, he plans and carries out the robbery in the tomb, and transports Callirhoe all the way to Asia Minor to separate her as much as possible from the people who might recognize her. His only goal in all these deeds is profit. Other characters who acted less than nobly did so for what they thought were good and compelling reasons: self-preservation, loyalty to a master, and fear.

Theron enters the scene at the funeral procession of Callirhoe, and he is amazed and made greedy by the sight of all the riches going to the grave with Callirhoe. To a man of Theron's sentimental nature, it must have seemed a felony to waste so much gold on a dead girl when there were so many living people willing to pay with their lives for it. His baser instincts aroused, Theron plots to rob the grave—even at night he plots because he can get no rest while thinking of the gold. If the old adage is true, and you can judge a man by his friends, Theron is a proper villain. His acquaintances have no compunctions about piracy, robbing tombs, or rifling temples. Nothing, including the lives of men or gods, are sacred to these men. Nor are they truly brave men. When they suspect a ghost in Callirhoe's tomb, they refuse to go into it; Theron has no such fears. Profit is the compelling motive in Theron's mind, and it is much greater there than in the minds of his cohorts. When his accomplices allow discretion to become the better part of valor and think it best to kill Callirhoe, because she is the only link between them and the tomb robbery, Theron vetoes the idea when the thought of selling her occurs to him. Again we have the profit motive. With all the confidence of a superswindler, he unloads his prize on an unsuspecting Leonas, pockets his reward, and flees the country without having to provide any bill of sale for Callirhoe.

Divine retribution finally catches up with Theron, the villain.

In Chariton's world, as in the world of Greeks for many centuries, men like Theron of overweening pride and audacity are struck down by divine agents, in this case the sea. In Greek myth and in literature built around myths, we discover that the sea plays an important part in many cases of divine retribution. Sometimes, as in the case of Theron, the punishment and retaliation by the divine powers of the universe result in the death of the villain. Chariton has singled out Theron as the archvillain in his novel in two ways: First, only in the episode built around Theron does Chariton employ the device of the *deus ex machina* to catch a wrongdoer. For Chariton this rhetorical device is spectacularly unusual and is surely used to call attention to the fact that the gods themselves have intervened to bring justice to earth. Except for the capture of Theron, Chariton writes only about affairs which originate and end on earth. Secondly, Chariton points to Theron as the archvillain by allowing him to be the only named character in this story to die. All other actors survive to the end. Not only does Theron die and die violently, but also cruelly. He is impaled or, as the original Greek has it, skewered.

A word or two in defense of Theron. Judged by today's standards he is a pale shadow of a real villain, a Hitler, a concentration camp commandant, or an officer at My Lai. In fact he is not a particularly villainous villain, but rather a common pirate, many of which must have plied the Mediterranean during Chariton's lifetime. Both his method of survival when his ship runs out of drinking water and his clever defense of himself at the court in Syracuse conspire to elicit our sympathies for him as a person and as a flesh-and-blood character on Chariton's stage.

III *Character Portrayal in Chariton*

Having gone through a character analysis of the minor roles in Chariton's novel and having provided an analysis of the major characters in the fourth chapter, we feel it appropriate to give also an overview of the ancient *ethopoiia* (character study) and rationale behind character portrayal and to note how Chariton applied it. For this study we have made use of Johannas Helms's *Character Portrayal in the Romance of Chari-*

ton (see the bibliography), available, unfortunately, in only the biggest and best libraries. In this work Helms differentiates four types of character portrayal: (1) Aristotelian dramatic characterization, which the great philosopher distilled from those Greek tragedies known to him; (2) forensic characterization, which is a highly specialized kind of character portrayal used by lawyers in the courtroom or by ghost writers for their paying customers to communicate a convincing and sympathetic character to the jury or audience; (3) Theophrastus's realistic characterization of types, which he wrote about in his tract entitled *Characters* (Theophrastus [d. 287 B.C.], a pupil of Aristotle, wrote on some thirty character types which are described and differentiated by a listing of various personal habits and reactions to specific events. We are left with thirty types and not one individual.); and (4) rhetorical characterization, which does not describe characters or what character portrayal should be, but concerns itself with theatrical displays of emotions and sentimental narrations.

For Chariton items one and four above apply most often; item three sometimes, and two never. While Helms is right in his analysis and provides illuminating comments on Aristotelian character portrayal, it is not necessary for Chariton to have known or followed these precepts for drawing characters. Chariton portrays characters in the same ways that the ancient Greek tragedians depicted their actors. Aristotle studied the tragedians and from that research determined the "correct" method of character delineation. We contend that Chariton learned about character portraiture from tragedy not from Aristotle. Elsewhere, we pointed out how much Chariton owed to the ancient tragedians (Chapter Two).

In the first place character is established by Chariton when his actors make moral choices to do or not to do something. Since the characters of Greek tragedy are morally good and are imitations of serious men, it is difficult to find a villain in tragedy. So it is with Chariton. Some characters are not as good as others but their intentions are honorable, even if the means they employ are not of the highest kind. Helms examines the depiction of the character-by-moral-choice on three levels: (1) third person comments; (2) revealing actions of the character; and (3) soul of the character revealed by his own speeches. By carefully manipulating the amount of third-person comment, whether made by Chariton as the narrator or by one of the actors, Chariton brings a kind of irony to the work because certain of the characters are unaware of what other characters and the readers know. This disparity of understanding leads to a fairly high level of irony. Since much of what the characters do is not to act but rather to react to situations, the second item above is not as important as the other two. Item three above is important because we learn much about character description from it. As in tragedy and epic, Chariton provides his actors with long monologues or dialogues (with confidants as an audience) which reveal the kind of souls possessed by each individual.

In the second place Chariton develops well-proportioned characters by adding just enough realism to his otherwise quite romantic and idealized actors to keep them in the familiar world. According to Aristotle, art forms like drama, and by extension Greek novels, should imitate life—Aristotle's famous *mimesis* theory. This is, of course, to point out the obvious. Theatregoers and readers of ancient fiction seem to prefer a blend of realism and idealism which helps them to reflect on the troubles of the day but gives them hope for the future. Chariton's characters clearly move in an ideal world which can never harm them permanently. Into this generally idealized world Chariton injects certain elements of realism to make his characters actors on a believable stage. Helms uses the techniques of Theophrastus in commenting on Chariton's character portrayal, and believes that Chariton may have had Theophrastus's *Characters* in the back of his mind when he created the actors that populate his novel. It seems clear, moreover, that Theophrastus got his characters from comedy, perhaps from playwrights like Menander (d. ca. 291 B.C.). (There is little validity to the story that Menander was a pupil of Theophrastus.) We believe that Chariton, a lover of the stage and things dramatic, also took his characters from the stage.

Chariton brings realism to his character portrayal by paying close attention to small details, color of hair, styles of clothes, private thoughts and daydreams, and personal emotions released in seclusion. His characters have pride, a sense of right and wrong, justified fears, and a propensity to jealousy; his actors have developed a system of ethics based on the situation and not entirely dependent on abstract ideals. When sudden news is brought to any character, he fears, like the rest of us, the worst. Chariton's characters are real because they are human.

Aristotle believed that a well-drawn character should have *internal* consistency. Theron begins as a villain, is a villain in the middle of his episode, and dies like a villain. From beginning to end Chariton's characters run true to form. Some of the characters, though, show development, which does not interfere with consistency. Chaereas is a worthy example of this. He is basically the same character at the beginning of the novel and at its conclusion. But he is a better-developed character, which is expected, and also a more mature person. On his trip through life he has learned something. At the same time that we in the audience learn more about Chaereas, we can observe that our continuum of facts and information is portraying a living and developing actor. The character and portrayal of Chaereas are not only consistent; they are alive and well.

While Chariton is perhaps guilty by our standards of making his characters conform too much to a type, he is less guilty than his successors in the genre. There is a conscious attempt in Chariton to create interesting and viable characters who control their own actions and who cause or generate many of the scenes and incidents which follow. Fate and Fortune govern a disproportionately large share of all incidents in Greek novels. In those prose fiction works which follow Chariton's, episodes and incidents supplant the development of character, and the reason for the existence of the novel becomes the creation of scenes of wonderment, shock, and pity.

CHAPTER 7

The Influence of
Chariton on Later Literature

AS we indicated at the outset, the influence of Chariton, and
in a way of all Greek romances, has not been great. The
causes for this are many, but two will suffice. First, those interested from the earliest time in Greek literature never took Chariton's work seriously. Greek romance never measured up when
compared with the literature of Periclean Athens. But this is to
compare meat and potatoes with *crêpes suzettes*. If one were to
make fifth-century Greece the standard, little perhaps of the
next two and one-half millennia would be comparable. The
second reason for Chariton's slight influence is the loss of his
manuscripts. Unlike Vergil, for instance, who has been known
and read continuously from his death to the present, Chariton
was virtually unknown from shortly after his death until 1750.

Chariton stepped out of darkness into the shade and dim
light when fragments of copies of his novel were found in
Egypt. Three fragments were uncovered, two of papyri and
one of parchment. In 1898 the German scholar Wilcken got
hold of several pages of a parchment (sheepskin) of the sixth
or seventh century A.D. from Thebes, on which was written a
section of Chariton's novel. It is fortunate that a man of Wilcken's
ability had found this manuscript, because the words of Chariton were hidden under a Coptic document, which at a later
date had been set on top of Chariton's novel. This was not an
infrequent phenomenon because of the cost of preparing sheepskin for use as a writing material. Such a manuscript on which
two works have been copied, one on top of the other, is called
a palimpsest.[1] Only one copy of this manuscript survives because
the original was destroyed in a tragic fire. The first of two
papyrus manuscripts from Egypt was found in the Fayum, con-
160

taining parts of three columns which represent Chapters 2 and 3 of Book 4. The date of this, based on the writing style, is not later than A.D. 150. It is only because of the extremely arid climate in Egypt that these papyri survive at all.[2] Later a second papyrus was unearthed at Oxyrhynchus, containing Chapters 3 and 4 of Book 2, dated to the late second century.[3] Chariton's work, written in the late first or very early second century, must have been highly popular to have been published in small Egyptian towns shortly after, or within one hundred years of, its composition.

In addition to Chariton's popularity in his own life or soon thereafter, he had at least a short-lived influence on other Greek romances, especially on Xenophon of Ephesus's *The Adventures of Anthia and Habrocomes,* written soon after Chariton's own work. Right from the beginning Xenophon borrows from Chariton: Anthia and Habrocomes meet in a religious procession of young people and they fall in love at first sight. After preliminary lovesickness they marry, only to sail away, be separated, and follow in the steps of Chaereas and Callirhoe. Xenophon borrows the burial scene of Anthia from the burial of Callirhoe and even includes a similar description of the riches of the tomb. Of the five Greek novels only in Chariton's and Xenophon's do the protagonists marry at the beginning of the story before their separations. Then too, Chariton and Xenophon fall less under the fatal influence of rhetoricians. In addition to imitating or borrowing episodes and scenes, Xenophon reproduces many of the details from Chariton and goes to such lengths that he frequently reflects the style and language of his senior writer in the field.[4]

This is one of the last significant instances we can document with any evidence of Chariton's later influence, but a careful review of all the later Greek novels reveals many episodic and stylistic borrowings. In the late third century after the composition of Heliodorus's work and the anonymous *Historia Apollonii Regis Tyri,* the genre of the Greek novel, or if you will, romance, disappears. Few things, however, disappear absolutely or leave no traces of influence. We believe this holds true also for Greek prose fiction. In all probability the advent of Christianity destroyed the genre:

A fitting epitaph for the Greek erotic romance was penned by Nietzsche: "Christianity," he says, "gave Eros poison to drink; he did not die of it, certainly, but degenerated to Vice."[5]

From Chariton's work to the last of the genre there is a high premium put on the faithfulness of the lovers involved. This concern extends to virginity in the work of Longus, Achilles Tatius, and Heliodorus. In Chariton and Xenophon the lovers marry early in the story, and struggle to remain faithful ever after. No one in the history of literature ever guarded her marriage vows more faithfully or with more vigor than Anthia in Xenophon's novel. Callirhoe had not been so devout in the first Greek novel, and in her second marriage, however bigamous, Chariton showed a realism not evident in Xenophon. In Longus's *Daphnis and Chloe* Daphnis loses his virginity, but he can be excused for the reason provided by Longus: he did not know what he was doing. Chloe perseveres to her lawful wedding night. In Heliodorus's novel the hero and heroine guard their virginities from other suitors and from each other until their marriage. Virginity is so important in Heliodorus that tests are administered to check on this vital condition or state. In Achilles Tatius the hero Cleitophon is excused from a virginity test, which he could not have passed. His wife-to-be was subjected to it and passed; his one-night girlfriend, Melite, cheated on the test and was erroneously certified as faithful. The condition of virginity was so desirable that it was worthwhile to spend the effort in testing for it.

The death of the genre of the Greek novel, which depended heavily on virginity and struggles to protect it, is possibly credited to the rise of realism which refused to subscribe to stories of virgins. This drive for realism, which in one aspect resulted in the death of virginity as an important segment of the plot, probably alienated the primary audience of the genre—the lower and middle classes. When this audience became Christianized, it insisted on virginity. It would be extremely interesting if we could trace the cult of virginity (and the cult of the Virgin) back to the Greek novel. In point of fact among the early Christian writings which have come down to us under the title of Pseudo-Clementine Literature are two epistles concerning the importance and value of virginity. Perhaps in a more serious age love stories by their very nature were considered too frivolous to merit reading. The last pagan emperor, Julian (A.D. 361-363), who ruled after some years of Christian emperors, inveighed against romantic novels because they were openly fictitious.

In very late antiquity or in the early Middle Ages, both Heliodorus and Achilles Tatius were thought to be bishops. It is difficult on moral grounds to see how Achilles Tatius could be considered a bishop; Heliodorus, on the other hand, wrote a "moral" novel. This evidence runs in the face of our theory that late Greek novels were rejected by their middle-class audiences of Christians for their lack of morality. We believe that the form of the ancient Greek novel died along with its virgin heroines. The reason for writing the novel, the tales of ordeals of virgins, had disappeared. The tales of virgins were now the domain of the Church. This small matter aside, the character of a man like Heliodorus was obviously devout in his adherence to pagan cults. Throughout his work he displayed a religiosity about life which in turn showed that he concerned himself more with matters of the "church" than with matters of the "flesh." It appears that the new Christian readers rejected the ancient Greek novelists; the novels were transformed into vehicles for propaganda (in a nice sense) for the new church; following these actions, the ancient Greek novelists were once again accepted as legitimate. To be legitimate, however, the ancient Greek novelists were transformed into bishops. When the church felt it could not fight a pagan power of whatever kind, it merely incorporated it. Witness the two pagan gods Silvanus and Silvester: when the church could not drive their cults out of rural areas, the church adopted them as Saints Silvanus and Silvester!

Philostratus, in the early third century A.D., apparently knew of Chariton, who must have had considerable influence on later writers, or Philostratus would not have been so concerned about maligning him. Photius, patriarch of Byzantium and resident literary critic of the ninth century A.D., does not mention Chariton, but recommends Achilles Tatius and Heliodorus as worthy of reading, though he is offended by the former's lack of propriety. In the ascetic age of the Christian church, which followed the first several centuries after its founding, the overwrought and hyperbolical virtue and chastity-virginity of the heroine in Greek romance appealed to both the simple and the academic mind. And so it is that Achilles Tatius and Heliodorus became the standards of Greek novels. Chariton, as Perry has pointed out in many of his writings, represents an earlier pagan culture before the complete takeover of the rhetoricians, before the loss of nerve in the Roman Empire, and before any influence of the Christian church began to be felt.

In the five Greek novels, plus the Latin *Historia Apollonii Regis Tyri,* we meet again and again unbelievable faithfulness on the part of separated wives and husbands and invincible chastity in the person of beautiful young lovers, who are confronted with tortures of all kinds if they do not yield to their opponents' passions. It is this element or motif of chastity in the face of strong passions which influences and shapes the hagiographic romances. Though many features of the ancient Greek novels can be seen in early Christian writings, the most dominant is that of virginity.

Other influences, especially in the area of motifs from Greek novels, are easily isolated. Early Christian hagiographic writings frequently embellished historical facts or outlines and fleshed them out with fictional materials intended to edify the reader. We see among the *Acts of the Christian Martyrs* and certain works like the *Martyrdom of Polycarp, Martyrdom of Pionius,* and the *Acts of Apollonius,* the blurring of the line between history and fiction. Christian literature also borrows the motif of the search for separated loved ones. In the Pseudo-Clementine *Recognitions* Clement travels from Rome to the East, accompanies Peter on his missionary journeys, and discovers his mother and twin brother (shades of New Comedy) living in the East. Aristotle referred to such a denouement as *anagnorisis.* The erotic love motif is obviously gone, but the love motif is nonetheless present.

Another major feature of ancient Greek novels which appears in early Christian narrative prose is the travel motif. It is stressed in the *Recognitions,* but in the *Peregrinatio Aetheriae* or *Journey of Aetheria* it is the dominant motif. Aetheria travels to the strange East and sends back tales of her marvelous adventures. Strictly defined, hagiographical documents are those writings of a religious character whose intent is to edify the reader. These writings must be inspired by a religious adoration of the early saints of the church:

> If the writer's aim is to depict the life and spirit of a saint honored by the Church by means of a series of happenings that are partly real and partly imaginary, then the work may be called a hagiographical romance. . . . Romances of this . . . kind are very numerous, and some of them go back to very early times: for example, the Acts of Paul and Thecla, and that collection of apocryphal Acts of the Apostles which had so long and remarkable a vogue. And there are the Clementine romances (Homilies and Recognitions).[6]

Perhaps Greek novels had their greatest influence, in every sense, on these early Christian edifying fictional narratives. Chariton virtually disappears until 1750 when Jacob D'Orville published a Greek edition, with accompanying Latin translation by J. Reiskius, based on a thirteenth-century manuscript in Florence. Until other manuscripts were found in Egypt, the text of Chariton rested on that single witness. Chariton's story was turned into English in 1764, and then not even from the original Greek but from an earlier Italian translation. And at this point the story of Chariton comes to a kind of end, a rather sad end, an indictment not of him but of us who refused to treat him seriously.

Notes and References

Chapter One

1. *Der griechische Roman und sein Vorläufer* (Wiesbaden: Breitkopf und Härtell, 1914).
2. *Greek Romances in Elizabethan Fiction* (New York: Columbia University Press, 1912).
3. The latest in a series of books: John Sullivan, *The Satyricon of Petronius: A Literary Study* (London: Faber and Faber, 1968). P. G. Walsh, *The Roman Novel* (Cambridge: Cambridge University Press, 1970).
4. *Longus* (New York: Twayne, 1970).
5. Berkeley: University of California Press, 1967.
6. A. Boeckh, *Corpus Inscriptionum Graecarum* (Berlin: Ex Officina Academia, 1843), vol. 2, no. 2846.
7. *Op. cit.,* 2748; 2782-2783.
8. Otto Weinreich, *Der griechische Liebesroman* (Zürich: Artemis, 1962), p. 13.
9. August, 1967, pp. 280-94; June, 1972, pp. 766-91.
10. *Zur Sprache Charitons* (Dissertation, Köln, 1963).
11. Wilhelm von Christ, *Geschichte der griechischen Literatur,*[6] newly edited by W. Schmid and O. Stählen. Zweiter Teil, Zweite Hälfte, von 100 bis 530 nach Christum (München: Beck, 1961), pp. 806 ff.

Chapter Two

1. *The Theory of the Leisure Class* (New York: Macmillan, 1912).
2. *The Ancient Romances,* p. 90.
3. J.P.V.D. Balsdon, *Life and Leisure in Ancient Rome* (London: The Bodley Head, 1969).
4. L. Friedländer, *Roman Life and Manners under the Early Empire,* vol. 3, tran. J. H. Freeze (London: Routledge, 1909), pp. 36-38.
5. R. P. Duncan-Jones, "Wealth and Munificence in Roman Africa," *Publications of the British School at Rome* 31 (1963), 159-71.
6. N. Lewis, *L'Industrie du Papyrus dans l'Egypte Gréco-Romaine* (Paris: Rodstein, 1934).

167

7. Peter Brunt, "Pay and Superannuation in the Roman Army," *Publications of the British School in Rome* 18 (1950), 50-71.

8. F. Cumont, "Non fui, fui, non sum," *Musée Belge* 32 (1928), 73-85. For more on pessimism in the first century A.D., see A. D. Nock, *Conversion* (Oxford: Oxford University Press, 1933), p. 272: "Further, the small man in antiquity suffered from a marked feeling of inferiority and from a pathetic desire for self-assertion, of which the epitaphs supply abundant illustration."

9. N. Frye, *Anatomy of Criticism* (New York: Atheneum, 1968), pp. 243 ff.

10. P. G. Walsh, *The Roman Novel*; Ben Perry, *The Ancient Romances*.

11. N. Frye, *Anatomy of Criticism*, pp. 303 ff.

12. Berne: A. Francke, 1946.

13. *The Ancient Romances*, pp. 18 ff.

14. B. Croce, *Aesthetics* (London: Macmillan, 1909) and R. K. Hack, "The Doctrine of Literary Forms," *Harvard Studies in Classical Philology* 27 (1916), 1-64.

15. *Recky Roman Dobrodruzny* (Prague: Filosofika Fakulta University Karlova, 1925).

16. New York: Oxford University Press, 1966.

17. *Institutio Oratoria* v. 11. 19.

18. Pliny *Epistulae* 2.20.1.

19. N. Frye, *Anatomy of Criticism*, pp. 243 ff.

20. *Ibid.*, p. 57.

21. A. B. Lord, *The Singer of Tales* (Cambridge: Harvard, 1960).

22. A. Scobie, *Aspects of Ancient Romance and its Heritage* (Meisenheim: Anton Hain, 1969), pp. 22-23.

23. E. Rohde, *Der griechische Roman*, p. 376; see also J. W. H. Walden, "Stage Terms in Heliodorus's *Aethiopica*," *Harvard Studies in Classical Philology* 5 (1894), 1-43.

24. B. Perry, *The Ancient Romances*, p. 141.

25. R. Reitzenstein, *Hellenistische Wundererzählungen* (Leipzig: Teubner, 1906), pp. 92-99.

26. See further E. Haight, *Essays on the Greek Romance* (New York: Longmans, 1943), pp. 26 ff.

27. M. Braun, *History and Romance in Graeco-Oriental Literature* (Oxford: Blackwell, 1938).

28. J. Barnes, "Egypt and the Greek Romance," *Akten des VIII. Internationalen Kongress für Papyrologie: Wien, 1955. Mitteilungen aus den Papyrussamlungen der österreichischen National Bibliothek* n.s. 5 (1956), 29-36.

29. Reported in Photius *Bibliotheca* 72.

30. F. W. Walbank, "History and Tragedy," *Historia* 9 (1960), 216-34.

31. Sir Ronald Syme, *The Roman Revolution* (Oxford: Oxford University Press, 1943).

32. "On the Origins of the Greek Romance," *Eranos* 60 (1962), 132-59.

33. *Ibid.*, 142.

34. S. Gaselee, ed., *Parthenius* (Cambridge: Harvard, 1916), p. 410.

35. *The Greek Novella in the Classical Period* (Cambridge: Cambridge University Press, 1958).

Chapter Four

1. Elizabeth Evans, *Physionomics in the Ancient World. Transactions of the American Philosophical Society* n.s. 59.5 (1969) *passim* and 73.

2. *National Geographic*, June, 1972, pp. 768-69.

3. See G. Steiner, "The Graphic Analogue from Myth in Greek Romance," *Classical Studies Presented to Ben Edwin Perry. Illinois Studies in Language and Literature* 58 (1969), 123-37.

4. *Exclusus Amator: A Study in Latin Love Poetry* (Madison: American Philological Association, 1956).

5. A. D. Nock, *Conversion*, p. 200.

6. See Henry Ormerod, *Piracy in the Ancient World* (Liverpool: Liverpool University Press, 1924).

7. On the widespread practice of abortion see W. Krenkel, "Erotica I: Der Abortus in der Antike," *Wissenschaftliche Zeitschrift der Universität Rostock* 20 (1971), 443-52.

8. T. M. Rattenbury, "Chastity and Chastity Ordeals in Ancient Greek Romances," *Proceedings of the Leeds Philosophical and Literary Society: Literature and History Section* 1 (1926), 63, so argues. He is mistaken.

Chapter Five

1. G. M. A. Grube, *The Greek and Roman Critics* (London: Methuen, 1968), p. 259.

2. Joseph Campbell, *The Hero With a Thousand Faces* (New York: World Publishing, 1956) [1949], p. 35.

Chapter Six

1. Sophocles: *A Study of Heroic Humanism* (Cambridge: Harvard, 1951).

2. N. Frye, *Anatomy of Criticism,* p. 57.

3. For a complete analysis of the hero along the above lines see Charles Moorman, *A Knyght There Was* (Lexington: University of Kentucky Press, 1967).

4. Jean Frappier, *Arthurian Literature in the Middle Ages* (Oxford: Oxford University Press, 1957).

5. William Woods, "The Plot Structure of Four Romances of Chrétien de Troyes," *Studies in Philology* 50 (1953), 4.

6. Joseph Campbell, *The Hero With a Thousand Faces,* pp. 245-46.

7. *Ibid.,* p. 193.

8. For certain of the ideas here we owe a debt of thanks to Charles Moorman, *A Knyght There Was.*

Chapter Seven

1. U. Wilcken, "Eine neue Romanhandschrift," *Archiv für Papyrusforschung* 1 (1901), 227-72.

2. B. Grenfell and A. Hunt, *Fayum Towns and Their Papyri* (London: Egypt Exploration Fund, 1900), pp. 74-82.

3. A. Hunt, *The Oxyrhynchus Papyri,* Part 7 (London: Egypt Exploration Fund, 1910), pp. 143-46.

4. F. Garin, "Su i Romanzi Greci," *Studi Italiani di Filologia Classica* 17 (1909), 423-60.

5. B. Perry, *The Ancient Romances,* p. 105.

6. H. Delehaye, *The Legends of the Saints* (London: Geoffrey Chapman, 1962), p. 5; see also A. D. Nock, *Conversion,* pp. 200 ff., and H. Musurillo, *Fathers of the Primitive Church* (New York: New American Library, 1966), pp. 24-25.

Selected Bibliography

Those students of ancient fiction interested in a definitive bibliography will find these classical journals and periodicals admirable in every respect.

ENGELMANN, W. *Bibliotheca Scriptorum Classicorum*, 2 vols. Leipzig: Reisland, 1880. Bibliography for 1700-1878.
KLUSSMANN, R. *Bibliotheca Scriptorum Classicorum*, 2 vols. Leipzig: Reisland, 1912. Bibliography for 1878-1896.
LAMBRINO, S. *Bibliographie de l'Antiquité Classique*. Paris: Les Belles Lettres, 1951. Bibliography for 1896-1914.
L'Année Philologique, journal of classical bibliographical information, published yearly under joint sponsorship of French and American scholarly organizations.
Jahresberichte über die Fortschritte der klassischen Altertumswissenschaft, succeeded in 1956 by *Lustrum,* both are journals of classical bibliographical information, published yearly by German scholars.

PRIMARY SOURCES

1. Greek Texts:

BLAKE, WARREN. *Charitonis Aphrodisiensis de Chaerea et Callirhoe libri octo.* Oxford: Clarendon Press, 1938. Best critical edition.
D'ORVILLE, JACOBUS. *Charitonis Aphrodisiensis libri octo.* Amsterdam: Mortier, 1750. First critical edition; Latin translation and copious notes.
HERCHER, R. *Erotici Scriptores Graeci. Charitonis Aphrodisiensis libri octo,* vol. 2. Leipzig: Teubner, 1859.

2. English Translations of Chariton:

BLAKE, WARREN. *Chariton's Chaereas and Callirhoe.* Ann Arbor: University of Michigan Press, 1938. Only one available. Extremely accurate, but very wooden and uninspiring.
BECKET, T. and DE HONDT, P. A: *The Loves of Chaereas and Callirhoe.* Written originally in Greek by Chariton, now first translated into English, 2 vols. London: 1764. Earliest English translation.

171

3. Italian and French Translations:

GIACOMELLI, MICHEL ANGELO. *Di Caritone Afrodisieo. De' racconti amorosi di Cherea e di Callirroe libri otto.* Rome, 1752, again in 1756; new edition in Parigi, 1781; new edition still in Italian in London: Richard Edward, 1792; new edition in Pisa, 1816.

CALDERINI, A. *Le avventure di Cherea e Calliroe,* Torino: Bocca, 1913.

LACHER, PIERRE HENRI. *Histoire des amours de Chereas et de Callirhoë,* 2 vols. Paris, 1763; new edition in the *Bibliothèque universelle des Dames: Romans,* tom. 6, 7, in Paris, 1785; new edition in Paris, 1797; reprinted in 1823.

FALLETT, M. *Les Aventures de Choerée et de Callirhoé.* Amsterdam, 1775.

4. Translations of Other Ancient Novels:

HADAS, MOSES. *Three Greek Romances: Longus's Daphnis and Chloe; Xenophon of Ephesus's Ephesian Tale; Dio Chrysostom's Hunters of Euboea.* New York: Doubleday, 1953.

TURNER, PAUL. *Longus's Daphnis and Chloe.* Harmondsworth: Penguin, 1968.

LAMB, W. *Heliodorus's Ethiopian Story.* London: Dent, 1961.

GASELEE, STEPHEN. *Achilles Tatius's Leucippe and Clitophon.* London: Heinemann, 1917.

SULLIVAN, JOHN. *Petronius's Satyricon.* Harmondsworth: Penguin, 1965.

LINDSAY, JACK. *Apuleius's The Golden Ass.* Bloomington: University of Indiana Press, 1962.

TURNER, PAUL. *Apollonius Prince of Tyre.* London: Golden Cockerel Press, 1956.

HAIGHT, ELIZABETH. *The Romance of Alexander.* New York: Longmans, 1954.

SECONDARY SOURCES

1. Studies in Chariton:

BARTSCH, WERNER. *Der Charitonroman und die Historiographie.* Dissertation: Leipzig, 1934. Bartsch claims that ancient romance grew out of Hellenistic historical forms.

BLAKE, WARREN. "Chariton's Romance—The First European Novel," *Classical Journal* 29 (1933–34), 284-88. Written in A.D. 150, Chariton's novel is the first of that genre.

CALDERINI, A. *Le Avventure di Cherea e Calliroe.* Torino: Bocca,

1913. Long and detailed study of Chariton's place in Greek literature. Best philological study of Chariton and his sources.

COBET, C. G. "Annotationes Criticae," *Mnemosyne* 8 (1859), 229-303. Philological analysis of Chariton's Greek.

GASDA, AUGUSTUS. *Quaestiones Charitoneae*. Dissertation: Breslau, 1860. Philological analysis of Chariton's language.

HELMS, J. *Character Portrayal in the Romance of Chariton*. The Hague: Mouton, 1966. Careful and detailed delineation of each character and type of character in the novel.

PAPANIKOLAOU, ANTONIOS. *Zur Sprache Charitons*. Dissertation: Köln, 1963. Chariton's Greek indicates that he lived and wrote before the Christian era.

PERRY, BEN. "Chariton and his Romance from a Literary-Historical Point of View," *American Journal of Philology* 51 (1930), 93-134. A study of character delineation, irony, and humor in Chariton.

PETRI, REMI. *Über den Roman des Chariton*. Meisenheim am Glan: Anton Hain, 1963. Unlike the other Greek romances, Chariton's work is not based on the rituals of mystery religions.

REIN, EDVARD. *Zum schematischen Gebrauch des Imperfekts bei Chariton*. Helsinki: Suomalaisen Tiedealatemian Toimikuksia, 1927. By linguistic analysis Rein determines that Chariton imitated the Greek of Herodotus, Thucydides, and Xenophon.

2. Studies in Ancient Romance Including Chariton:

BARNES, JOHN. "Egypt and the Greek Romance," *Mitteilungen aus den Papyrussammlungen der österreichischen National Bibliothek* n.s. 5 (1956), 29-36. Chariton is influenced by writers whose traditions go back to Alexandrian Egypt.

BRAUN, MARTIN. *History and Romance in Graeco-Oriental Literature*. Oxford: Blackwell, 1938. Greek Romance develops from more unsophisticated Egyptian Romances.

GIANGRANDE, G. "On the Origins of the Greek Romance," *Eranos* 60 (1962), 132-59. Alexandrian love-elegies are the source and origin of Greek Romance.

HELM, RUDOLF. *Der antike Roman*. Göttingen: Vandenhoeck and Ruprecht, 1956. Review of Greek and Latin Romances.

HAIGHT, ELIZABETH. *Essays on Ancient Fiction*. New York: Longmans, 1936. Readable essays on ancient novels.

————. *More Essays on Greek Romance*. New York: Longmans, 1945.

LAVAGNINI, BRUNO. *Le Origini del Romanzo Greco*. Pisa: Mariotti,

1921. Greek Romances arise in humble surroundings, based on popular local legends and myths.

McCulloh, William. *Longus.* New York: Twayne, 1970. A study of Longus's use of his Greek predecessors, and Longus's influence on later writers.

Merkelbach, Reinhold. *Roman und Mysterium.* München: Beck, 1962. Greek Romance has its origin in the ritual of Greek mystery religions.

Mittelstadt, M. C. "Love, Eros, and Poetic Language in Longus," *Fons Perennis: Saggi Critici di Filologia Classica raccolti in onore del. Prof. Vittorio D'Agostino.* Torino: Baccola and Gili, 1971, pp. 305-32. Longus adapts Greek pastoral poetry to the new forms of romance.

Perry, Ben. *The Ancient Romances: A Literary-Historical Account of their Origins.* Berkeley: University of California Press, 1967. The single best book on the rise of prose fiction in antiquity. A sound grasp of the nature of Greek Romance.

Phillimore, J. S. "The Greek Romances," in *English Literature and the Classics,* edited by C. S. Gordon. Oxford: Oxford University Press, 1912, pp. 87-117. Greek romance is a product of a senile people, not of a mature civilization.

Rattenbury, R. M. "Chastity and Chastity Ordeals in the Ancient Greek Romances," *Proceedings of the Leeds Philosophical and Literary Society: Literary and History Section* 1 (1926), 59-71. When Greek Romance no longer portrayed chaste heroines, the genre died.

————. "Romance: Traces of Lost Greek Novels," in *New Chapters in the History of Greek Literature,* edited by J. U. Powell. Oxford: Oxford University Press, 1933, pp. 211-57. Scholars must search early Egyptian writings for the sources of Greek Romance.

Reardon, B. P. "The Greek Novel," *Phoenix* 23 (1969), 291-309. The age of the Greek Romance is the age of the professional writer, prose fiction, and the rise of the individual.

Rohde, E. *Der griechische Roman und seine Vorläufer.* Leipzig: Breitkopf und Härtel, 1914. Before Perry, the best study of Greek Romance. Now much out of date. Excellent survey of the literary borrowings by Greek Romance writers from earlier Greek works.

Schwartz, E. *Fünf Vorträge über den griechischen Roman.* Berlin: De Gruyter, 1943. A study of narrative literature in Greece; emphasis on the historical side of Greek Romance.

Scobie, Alexander. *Aspects of the Ancient Romance.* Meisenheim am Glan: Anton Hain, 1969. A study, particularly in Apuleius, of paradoxography. A brief history of the rise and importance of the Greek novel.

STEINER, GRUNDY. "The Graphic Analogue from Myth in Greek Romance," *Classical Studies Presented to Ben Perry*. Urbana: University of Illinois Press, 1969, pp. 123-37. The use of myth in Romance.

TRENKNER, SOPHIE. *The Greek Novella in the Classical Period*. Cambridge: Cambridge University Press, 1958. The adaptation of folktales and indigenous Greek stories as motifs in New Comedy and Greek Romance.

TURNER, PAUL. "Novels, Ancient and Modern," *Novel* 2 (1968), 15-24. The genre of the novel first appeared in Greece in the first century A.D., not in England in 1700. A defense of the quality of Greek novels.

WALSH, P. G. *The Roman Novel*. Cambridge: Cambridge University Press, 1970. An analysis of the mixed forms which led to the creation of the *Satyricon* and the *Metamorphoses*. Parenthetical statements about Greek novels.

WEINREICH, OTTO. *Der griechische Liebesroman*. Zürich: Artemis, 1962. Short history of Greek Romance, particularly stressing Heliodorus.

WOLFF, SAMUEL. *The Greek Romances in Elizabethan Prose Fiction*. New York: Columbia University Press, 1912. The influence of certain Greek Romances on early English writers of fiction.

Two books unavailable for this study should be cited here: Tomas Hägg, *Narrative Technique in Ancient Greek Romances*. Stockholm: Acta Instituti Atheniensis Regni Sueciae, VIII, 1971; and Karl Kerenyi, *Der Antike Roman*. Darmstadt: Wissenschaftliche Buchgesellschaft, 1971.

Index